S0-AEA-706

WADSWORTH ENGLISH FOR ACADEMIC PURPOSES SERIES

Charles H. Blatchford and Jerry L. Messec, Series Editors

Available in 1987

Academically Speaking Janet Kayfetz and Randy Stice

Academic Writing Workshop Sarah Benesch, Mia Rakijas, and
    Betsy Rorschach

Overheard and Understood Sharon Bode and Sandra Moulding Lee

Understanding Conversations Catherine Tansey and Charles H.
    Blatchford

Academic Writing Workshop

Sarah Benesch
College of Staten Island, CUNY

Mia Rakijas
Hunter College, CUNY

Betsy Rorschach
City College, CUNY

Wadsworth Publishing Company
Belmont, California
A Division of Wadsworth, Inc.

English/ESL Editor: John Strohmeier
Series Editors: Charles H. Blatchford and Jerry L. Messec
Editorial Associate: Holly Allen
Production Editor: Vicki Friedberg
Interior and Cover Designer: Andrew H. Ogus
Print Buyer: Karen Hunt
Copy Editor: Pat Tompkins
Compositor: Kachina Typesetting
Cover Photographer: Ed Young

© 1987 by Wadsworth, Inc. All rights reserved. No part of this book may be reproduced, stored in a retrieval system, or transcribed, in any form or by any means, electronic, mechanical, photocopying, recording, or otherwise, without the prior written permission of the publisher, Wadsworth Publishing Company, Belmont, California 94002, a division of Wadsworth, Inc.

Printed in the United States of America

1 2 3 4 5 6 7 8 9 10—91 90 89 88 87

Library of Congress Cataloging-in-Publication Data

Benesch, Sarah.
Academic writing workshop.

   (The Wadsworth English for academic purposes series)
   1. English language—Text-books for foreign speakers.
I. Rakijas, Mia. II. Rorschach, Betsy. III. Title.
IV. Series.
PE1128.B446 1987   808'.042   86.28156
ISBN 0-534-07560-6

Contents

Chapter 2/Introductions 14

UNIT TWO/
DEVELOPING WRITING STRATEGIES 31

Chapter 3/First Impressions 32

Chapter 4/Observations 44

Chapter 5/Revising 59

Chapter 6/Research   75

Chapter 7/Editing   92

UNIT THREE/ WRITING ABOUT READING 105

Chapter 8/Taking Notes 106

Chapter 9/Summaries 117

Chapter 10/Short Essay 123

About the Wadsworth EAP Series

The Wadsworth English for Academic Purposes (EAP) series was conceived to provide appropriate teaching materials for college courses that focus on the academic uses of English. The eighteen texts of the EAP series are designed to help ESL students achieve communicative competence in all aspects of academic life in the United States. These materials teach the skills of reading, writing, listening, and speaking, and can be used for either intensive or nonintensive formats, in classrooms or for individual study, and for courses of varying lengths.

The Wadsworth EAP series is based on three principles:

1. *Comprehensive skills development:* Because the EAP program is based on the philosophy that language is an integrated unity, each book not only stands on its own but also prepares for and builds on other texts in the series. Individual skills are explored in depth at three distinct levels of proficiency; topics across all skill levels retain a consistent yet nonrepetitive approach.

2. *Academic community context:* The Wadsworth EAP series prepares students for the varied language uses they will encounter daily in their academic careers. All teaching and learning activities are set in the context of college or university classes; however, some texts go even further to depict the extended academic community. This context-specific approach assumes that students possess the learning skills and educational background typically found at academic English centers.

3. *Student-centered, process-oriented materials:* Each text in the Wadsworth EAP series places student learning activities at the heart of each lesson, requiring students to take an active responsibility for their role in the learning process.

The components of the Wadsworth EAP program will include:

Three grammar practice books that encourage students to practice language appropriate to specific academic contexts.

Six listening comprehension texts and tapes that develop (a) listening skills to the level needed for achievement in an academic program and (b) appreciation of the social situations students will experience in the extended academic community.

Three oral language books whose progressive communicative activities develop the spoken language skills necessary for students in U.S. campus communities.

Three reading skill development books that help students acquire skills for reading authentic English texts within the academic community context.

Three progressive process-oriented writing texts that develop writing skills from practice with the Latin alphabet (for those unfamiliar with the system) to communicative writing to writing based on individual research. Writing assignments are based on both visual and written situations. Higher-level texts provide instruction and practice in summarizing articles and research as well as in preparing longer papers. All three books combine practice in composing and editing to the degree necessary to express ideas logically and clearly.

The authors of the Wadsworth EAP series have developed their materials based on teaching experience, but the series is not teacher-proof; it will not work for someone who expects all the answers and a strict step-by-step approach. Each text is designed to allow instructors the flexibility to use their own teaching schemes, styles, and techniques. Not providing all "correct" answers reflects current trends in ESL teaching, which focus on the student as a developing being, struggling to construct, to decipher, and to negotiate meaning. Some texts do provide answer keys, however, as a help to students who may be using the text on their own.

Although no textbook is ideal for all students (or all teachers), this program will work for everyone who is willing to participate fully in classes and assignments. The texts are intended to broaden the students' vision and empower them with the expanding possibilities of language. Control and support are found not only in the materials themselves, but also in the teachers who guide the students through them. Just as students can learn to make language their servant, so can instructors learn to make the materials support their individual pedagogical goals.

In sum, the Wadsworth EAP series does more than simply prepare students for a grammar-based examination; the program can help international students master communication in academic English through meaningful practice in the American academic context. The student-centered materials shift the responsibility for learning from the teacher to the student, who, in the process, is provided the opportunity to fulfill his or her potential. And isn't that what each of us would like to achieve?

Charles H. Blatchford and Jerry L. Messec,
Series Editors

Acknowledgments

This book went through many stages over the course of several years, from initial idea to final version. We would like to thank all the people who helped us at the various stages:

—Lil Brannon, who got us started on the project and provided feedback and inspiration

—Our students at New York University, College of Staten Island, Hunter College, and LaGuardia Community College, who generously allowed us to use their work as examples of ESL students' writing and revising

—John Mayher, Nancy Lester, Lynn Goldstein, and Elaine Brooks, who read and commented extensively on drafts of the manuscript

—Jane Benesch, Jersey Gilbert, and Peter Oberlink, who wrote clear articles on difficult subjects for us to use as readings

—William Biddle, Harvard University; Ed Demerly, Henry Ford Community College; and Keith Pharis, Southern Illinois University, who reviewed the manuscript for Wadsworth

Finally, we would like to thank our editors, Charley Blatchford, Jerry Messec, and Jean Dale, as well as the Wadsworth staff—John Strohmeier, Vicki Friedberg, and Andrew Ogus—who understood and supported our ideas and helped turn the manuscript into a book.

Introduction to Teachers

Academic Writing Workshop is a beginning-level text that will help ESL students write for college courses. The chapters in Units 1 and 2 introduce students to the terminology of the writing process and have them practice strategies that will help them begin writing (invention and first draft writing), continue writing (revision), and finish writing (editing). The chapters in Unit 3 emphasize that writing is a tool students can use to help themselves learn. Assignments in Units 1 and 2 are designed to help students learn how to write in English, while those in Unit 3 have been modeled after the types of writing students are typically asked to do in U.S. academic institutions. Academic writing involves writing descriptions and observations, explanations of processes, and research reports. In addition, academic writing entails taking notes, summarizing, and using writing to think and learn. All of these will be practiced by ESL students as they work through this book.

Equally important for beginning-level ESL students as the need to learn academic writing is the need to become comfortable with writing in English. For these students especially, anxiety about their ability to produce correct written English is almost overwhelming, and they believe that they do not know enough English to be able to write at all. To help these students become less self-conscious and more assured when writing, we have designed the book to begin with freewriting exercises and with Academic Journal writing. The freewriting and Academic Journal writing will help them see that writing is not a matter of getting everything correct the first time it appears on paper, but rather a matter of first getting the ideas down where they can look at and then revise them. The freewriting and Academic Journal writing will also help reassure these students that indeed they can write English and that their proficiency with the language will improve as they write more.

The Process Approach

Central to all the writing assigned in this book is the *process approach*, whose main tenet is that writing is a process of generating ideas, drafting, getting feedback, revising, and editing. Experienced writers know that a piece of writing evolves from early tentative versions to the final polished draft. Most students, though, think that finished pieces of writing flow magically from pen to paper at the first attempt, and so they are frustrated when they have trouble knowing what and how to write.

Throughout the book, students will have many opportunities to experience the process of finding topics, exploring ideas in writing, giving and receiving feedback, and revising. By the time the students reach Chapter 7, in which they will edit their final drafts, they will have written and revised many short pieces of writing without having had to concern themselves with spelling, punctuation, and usage. To delay editing until pieces of writing have gone through invention, drafting, and revising is a basic principle of the process approach. Research in composing has demonstrated that when writers are concerned with editing early in the composing process they become so involved with getting the language right that they neglect the ideas. We have, therefore, given students plenty of time and occasions for writing and revising without asking them to edit immediately. For learners of a second language, this delay in editing is particularly important. These students tend to be overly sensitive to correctness and need to be given strategies that stress the early stages of the writing process. Their early drafts should be imperfect rehearsals for their more polished final drafts.

Small Group Work

Along with generating ideas, drafting, revising, and editing, students will work with one another in pairs or small groups. They will "share" and "respond" in their groups. "Sharing" is reading one's writing aloud to others, and "responding" is giving and receiving feedback about drafts-in-progress (see Chapter 4). Small groups provide students with an audience for their writing-in-progress. Sharing provides them with the reassurance that their peers are struggling with writing as much as they. Each group member learns that writing is difficult for everyone. Small groups take student writers out of their isolation and bring them into contact with fellow writers who are also trying to fulfill assignments and develop their ideas in writing.

Writing Assignments in This Book

Each chapter in this book includes Academic Journal, in-class, and at-home writing assignments.

The Academic Journal is not a journal in the traditional sense; that is, it is not a diary of intimate experiences. Instead, it is a notebook in which students write frequently for a variety of purposes without attention to correcting errors.

For students, the Academic Journal is a place to try out ideas in writing, jot down reactions to the class and the writing assignments, maintain an ongoing vocabulary list, take notes, and keep track of their own development as writers. For you, the Academic Journal is a monitoring device. Because you will periodically collect and read your students' Academic Journals, as indicated in each chapter, you will be able to check students' progress and respond to their writing. And, because you will comment in writing after some of the students' journal entries, you will engage in an ongoing, one-to-one dialogue with your students, a dialogue about ideas that is free from judgment and admonition about faulty language use.

Instruct students to begin this dialogue with you by having them mark those entries they want you to read and respond to. We have included sample teacher comments to journal entries in Chapter 1 in order to suggest a strategy for responding, but you should feel free to use your own response techniques as well. However, since freewriting and Academic Journal writing serve to promote fluency, we would caution against correcting them.

In this book, students are also instructed to do some writing in class and other writing at home. In-class writing assignments may be done at home and at-home assignments may be done in class. Assignments requiring group work must be done in class.

We do, however, want to emphasize the importance of writing in class. It helps to counteract the loneliness of writing and should therefore be encouraged. Create a community of writers in the classroom by bringing in your own work-in-progress and writing along with your students.

Other Features

As students complete in-class writing assignments, response sheets, progress charts, and at-home writing assignments, they should place their work in a Writing Folder. Any kind of folder that is at least 8½ by 11 inches will do.

The Writing Folder will help students keep their work together and organized. Students should not throw away any of their writing; they should keep together everything that is related to one paper—drafts, notes, response sheets, and so on—in their Writing Folders. Students will occasionally turn in their folders to you for diagnosis, response, or evaluation, as indicated throughout this book.

The four language tales in this book serve two functions: (1) they are entertaining to read and (2) they introduce important issues related to writing and language use. Students should read the language tales and share their reactions with the whole class. Since various interpretations of the tales are possible, class discussions will probably reveal differing opinions on the issues in question.

Class discussions about the language tales can serve as a springboard for writing, too. For example, the student text in Appendix B is a response to an assignment that asked students to write an ending to the language tale in Chapter 2.

We have found that students appreciate the opportunity to trade English words and phrases with classmates and to clarify their understanding of new vocabulary. For this reason we have included brief in-class vocabulary exercises in several chapters. These exercises will also help you make sure that students are keeping track of new words in their Academic Journal.

Diagnosing Students' Writing Problems

Even before you receive Writing Folders from your students for the first time (Chapter 4), look for certain signs as you watch your students write in class. Does a student pause, cross out, or erase a lot? Does a student use the dictionary frequently? Does a student ask, "What should I write?" Is the student's paper noticeably shorter than his classmates' papers? A combination of several of these signs may indicate writer's anxiety.

The work in students' Writing Folders will help you complete your diagnoses. Here are some suggestions for what to look for as you read through their work:

—Level of language ability
—Comprehensibility
—Control of idea

—Connectedness of ideas
—Inability to follow assignment directions (may indicate a reading problem)
—Length
—Problems with orthography
—Problems with spelling
—Recurring usage errors

The Writing Questionnaire, which students fill out in Chapter 1 and put in their Writing Folders, will also provide clues to the students' attitudes toward and experiences with writing.

Your in-class observations and assessment of students' early written work will help you determine what to work on in class to supplement the in-class writing assignments and small group meetings that are such an integral part of this book.

Responding to Students' Writing

Responding to students' writing may be the most demanding part of a writing teacher's job. Writing teachers want their comments to promote change and to encourage students to continue writing. ESL writing teachers feel extra responsibility because they believe they must deal simultaneously with their students' errors and ideas. The difficulty of their task makes writing teachers wish for a magic formula for responding to student writing that works every time for every student. Of course, such a formula does not exist. Each student draft is unique, with its own set of strengths and weaknesses. Each student has his own abilities and needs. And, as the student's teacher prepares to respond to his draft, she must take all these particularities into account. Therefore, an all-purpose response strategy is impossible to construct.

Here, however, are some general guidelines to keep in mind as you respond to students' drafts-in-progress (we have indicated in the book when you are expected to respond).

General Guidelines

—Tell the student what you understood from his draft. This will allow the writer to know what his writing communicated to a reader.
—Keep your comments "text-specific"; that is, refer to specific parts of the student's text. Comments such as "too general" and "unclear," for example, do not indicate which portion of the student's text might be perceived as too general or unclear and

why. Even a positive comment such as "Great idea!" is not as helpful as one that also explains which idea seems so good and why. (See Chapter 5 for an example of text-specific comments on a student draft.)

—In early drafts, point out usage problems only when they interfere with meaning.

—Don't overwhelm students with too many comments. Keep the revising process manageable.

—Remember that once you have made your comments it is the students' responsibility to act on them. Don't expect that they will incorporate all your comments in their revisions.

For a model of response to student writing, see Appendix B, which contains a student's first draft with his teacher's comments toward revision and a brief analysis of the text with an explanation of the teacher's comments.

Usage Problems

In Chapter 7 the students begin to edit their writing. Because student writers are better editors when they have specific things to edit for, the exercises in Chapter 7 have them look for only six problems: subject-verb agreement, verb tense, spelling, punctuation, capitalization, and articles. These are areas where beginning ESL writers frequently make errors, but you can expand this list, or make substitutions, to meet the needs of your class.

The list of editing problems is short for two reasons. First, editing is a difficult task; it takes time and a trained eye. Keeping a short editing list makes the task more manageable for beginning writers, and they will be more likely to check their text for each item on a brief list. As they become more adept at finding errors, the list can be lengthened or changed. Second, because this is a beginning-level writing course, students who can successfully edit for these six problems are doing well.

After students edit their own and their peers' drafts, you can check their corrections to make sure that they've edited properly.

Evaluating Student Writing

To use this book you do not need to implement any special system of evaluation. Most traditional methods of grading student writing—letter grades, percentages, pass/fail, and so on—can be easily integrated into the procedures specified in the chapters. We recommend, however, that you do not grade drafts-in-progress but evaluate only the final edited drafts of papers.

There are alternatives to grading final drafts as you receive them. One is to read every final edited draft as you receive it but defer grading until the end of your semester or session and then grade all the final edited drafts at the same time. Another is to read every final draft as you receive it and at the end of the semester or session ask students to choose the three or four final edited drafts they would like you to grade; then grade only those chosen final edited drafts.

Examples of Student Writing

The examples of ESL student writing throughout this book are at a level of ability perhaps higher than you should expect from your own students. It may be that not all of your students will write as much as appears in the examples. Please keep in mind, too, that except for the texts in the chapter on editing (Chapter 7), all of the student texts have been edited. Beginning-level students should not be expected to produce such grammatically perfect texts.

Assignments are preceded by examples of student writing that were triggered by those assignments. These examples serve as models for the users of this book. You and your students will be instructed to read and discuss the models before students fulfill the assignments.

To alleviate the problem of gender reference to teachers, we have alternated pronouns in the chapters of this book. In the odd-numbered chapters, teachers are referred to as *she;* in the even-numbered chapters, teachers are referred to as *he.*

Introduction to Students

All students write. They take notes from readings and from lectures. They write summaries and essays. This writing is called "academic writing." Academic writing can also be called "writing to learn." Taking notes and writing summaries and essays about history, biology, computer science, English, and other academic disciplines can help you understand and learn the subject matter more fully.

Writing Process

The questions students ask most often about writing are:

—Where do I get ideas to begin writing?
—How can I continue writing?
—How can I complete and correct a piece of writing?

Academic Writing Workshop will help you work on these questions by showing you ways to start writing, keep writing, read your writing, show your writing to other students and your teacher, talk about your writing, change your writing, and finally correct your writing. Notice that you will correct your writing at the *end* of this process.

How to Use This Book

Academic Writing Workshop invites you to write in class and at home, for yourself, your teacher, and your classmates. You will keep an Academic Journal for some assignments and a Writing Folder for other assignments. Sometimes you will sit in a small group with other students and read your writing out loud. At other times, your teacher will read your writing and give you feedback. So, in this writing textbook, you will be given many opportunities to read, listen to, and talk about your own and other peoples' writing.

Throughout the book you will find examples of student writing. Some of these examples are notes or lists; others are uncorrected pieces of writing (drafts); others are finished and corrected pieces of writing (edited drafts). You will read these examples before you do your own in-class or at-home writing. The examples of student writing may give you ideas for doing your own writing.

Each chapter has three types of writing assignments: In-Class Practice, At-Home Practice, and Academic Journal Practice. In addition, in some chapters you will find Progress Charts, Response Sheets, Language Tales, and Writing Questionnaires. All of these assignments will be explained before you begin to write.

UNIT ONE

Starting to Write

One of the difficulties of writing is knowing how to begin. In the first two chapters, you will do activities to help you begin to write. You will also talk, read, and write with your classmates.

CHAPTER 1

Academic Journals

In this chapter

—You will begin an Academic Journal. Scientists, artists, writers, musicians, and students write in their journals. They write in their journals to remember ideas and to solve problems.

—You will fill out a Writing Questionnaire. This questionnaire will help you look at your writing habits.

Buy a notebook. This notebook will be your Academic Journal. Write in your journal every day. Do not worry about making mistakes. Your teacher will collect your Academic Journal every few weeks. She will write comments under some of the entries. But your teacher will not correct your journal writing. Your journal is a place to write freely.

Here are some examples from Maria's Academic Journal. Under the entries from 2/16 and 2/21 there are comments from her teacher.

2-16

Translation is my biggest problem. I always use the dictionary. This makes writing very slow. What can I do?

Maria, I understand your difficulty.
You want to use the dictionary to
look up words, but this slows down
your writing. Try to write without
the dictionary. You can write some
words in your native language.
Later you can go back and look
them up in the dictionary.

2-21

The other students in the class know more
English. They studied for many years. They
have many ideas for writing, and they
write fast.

Maria —
Writing is difficult for everyone -
even natives. You will learn to
write by writing more and more.
Do you write in your native
language?

2-29

What is a group? Groups could be a
noun or verb. A group could be a set
of people, things, ideas, etc. To group is
to gather and put similar or different
things, people, places etc into a set.
Group is a mathematical term.

3-3

Today's class was good. I read my paper

5

to Ling. she liked it, but she didn't understand the end. I will change it and read it to her again. Her paper was good, but too short.

Start an Academic Journal

Divide your journal into three sections. Section 1 is for:

— "Thinking" on paper (Maria thought on paper about the word *group* in her entry from 2/29)
— Jotting down ideas
— Asking questions (Maria asked her teacher a question in her entry from 2/16 and her teacher answered)
— Writing about American culture and learning English (see Maria's entry from 2/21)
— Writing about the class (Maria wrote about her class in her entry from 3/3)

Section 2 is for vocabulary. Section 3 is for taking notes.

Academic Journal Practice: Section 1

1. Write your class schedule.
2. Write the name, address, and phone number of a classmate.
3. Write about today's class. What happened?
4. Write questions for your teacher about the class or about your school.

Write the date above each entry. Leave space between entries for your teacher's comments.

Record New Words

You can also keep a vocabulary list in your Academic Journal. Jan does. He adds new words to his list. First he writes the words. Next he writes where he read or heard them. Then he writes what he thinks they mean. Last he looks up the words in his dictionary. Here is part of Jan's vocabulary list:

word	where did I read or hear it?	what do I think it means?	dictionary definition
entry entries	in my writing textbook	the writing in a journal	" the act of coming or going in — the act or result of writing something down."
pre-requisite	in college catalog	pre = before prerequisite =?	"Something that is necessary before something else can happen or be done."
bursar's office	College catalog	a place to go in school to pay money	bursar = " a person in a college or school who is in charge of money."
interest	in the bank	something about money	" money paid for the use of money"
data base	on TV show about computers	something about computers	data = facts, information data base = ?

Jan easily understood *entry*, *bursar*, and *interest*. But *prerequisite* was a difficult word, and Jan wasn't able to understand it. He looked in the dictionary for *prerequisite* and found the definition. He wrote down the definition, but he did not understand it. He asked his teacher to explain *prerequisite*. She told him, "A prerequisite is a course that you must take before you can take a more advanced course. For example, Calculus 101 is a prerequisite for Calculus 201." Jan then understood *prerequisite*.

Jan looked in the dictionary for the definition of *data base*. But the word was not there. A student in Jan's math class knew a lot about computers. He told Jan, "*Data base* is all the information a computer files and keeps."

Use Section 2 of your Academic Journal for a vocabulary list. In this section, write down all new words you read or hear. Write where you read or heard them and what you think they mean. Then look them up in the dictionary. Use an English-English dictionary for learners of English (such as *Longman's*). If you don't find a word in the dictionary, ask your teacher or someone else.

Academic Journal Practice: Section 2

Start your vocabulary list. List five new words. You will use these words in the next in-class practice.

In-Class Practice: Vocabulary Exercise A

1. Each student chooses one or two new words from her Academic Journal and tells them to the teacher. The teacher writes the words on the board. Which words do you know? What do they mean? Tell the class. The teacher will write the definitions on the board.
2. Copy the words from the board onto the Vocabulary Exercise Chart. Copy the definitions, too.

Academic Journal Practice: Section 2

Copy Vocabulary Exercise Chart A into the vocabulary section of your Academic Journal.

Vocabulary Exercise Chart A

Word   *Definitions*

_____   _____

                           _____

                           _____

                           _____

_____   _____

                           _____

                           _____

                           _____

_____   _____

                           _____

                           _____

                           _____

_____   _____

                           _____

                           _____

                           _____

_____   _____

                           _____

                           _____

                           _____

Jot Down Ideas

You will get in-class and at-home writing assignments in all the chapters of this book. But sometimes you will have to make up your own assignments. So, whenever you have an idea for a paper, jot it down in Section 1 of your Academic Journal.

Choosing "My Own Topic"

1. Turn to the first section of your Academic Journal. Make a list of five writing topics. Look at Maria's list first:

   1. how to meet people
   2. the way American students dress
   3. study habits of American students
   4. my English courses in my country
   5. why I want to be a doctor.

2. Now, look at your list and choose *one* topic. What do you want to write about that topic? Make a list. In Chapters 2 and 3 you will write more about your topic.

Maria chose "The way American students dress." She wrote this about her topic:

   1. They dress very informally
   2. the professors don't mind
   3. In my country students dress formally

Ongoing Academic Journal Practice: Sections 1 and 2

1. Keep adding new words to Section 2.
2. Keep jotting down ideas for papers in Section 1.
3. After each class meeting, write about your class in Section 1. What happened? What did you learn? What questions do you have?

Remember to write the date above each entry. Remember to leave space between entries for your teacher's comments.

Writing Questionnaire 1:
Attitudes and Experiences

Name

Date

Answer these questions. Write your answers on this page. Then discuss
your answers with your classmates.

1. Do you like to write?

2. Why or why not?

3. What kinds of writing do you do in English?

4. What kinds of writing do you do in your native language?

Language Tale 1

When she was eight years old, Kachina was reading aloud to her mother. She saw *No. 59* and read, "No fifty-nine." Her mother explained, "When *no* is followed by a period, it means *number*." Two weeks later, Kachina was reading aloud from her book in class. She saw *No. No.* and said, "Number. Number." Her teacher asked, "Why did you say *number?*" Kachina answered, "Because when *no* is followed by a period, it means *number*." Her teacher smiled and then explained, "When *no* is followed by a period *and* a number, it means *number*. Here, it means *no.*" Kachina felt embarrassed, but she laughed at her mistake.

Some people say, "Making mistakes is a necessary part of learning a language." What do you think? Discuss this statement in class.

Summary

In this chapter you began an Academic Journal. You divided it into three sections. Section 1 is for thinking on paper, jotting down ideas, asking questions, writing about American culture and learning English, and writing about the class. Section 2 is your vocabulary list. Section 3 is for taking notes. You will begin Section 3 in Chapter 4.

CHAPTER 2

Introductions

In this chapter

—You will begin putting your in-class and at-home writing into a folder.

—You will write about yourself and about some of the people in your class.

—You will make lists and write descriptions from those lists. List making is one way to begin writing.

Get a folder for your in-class and at-home writing. This folder is a place to save all your writing. Tear out Writing Questionnaire 1 from Chapter 1 and put it in your folder.

Make Lists

Making a List

A *list* is a series of related words or phrases.

People write lists to collect their ideas and to remember.

Writers sometimes make lists to begin writing. They write words down or across the page. They don't worry about writing whole sentences. Later they choose words from their list and continue writing.

Describe Your Class

Nicolas looked at the people and things in his classroom. Then he wrote a list:

the teacher's desk and chair
the teacher
students' desks and chairs (25)
22 students
posters of places in the U.S.
A "No Smoking" sign
3 large windows
1 blackboard
A door
A map of the world

Nicolas used the information on his list to describe his class:

My classroom is on the third floor of Smith Hall. The room has 3 large windows. There are 22 students in the class. I don't know anyone's name. We sit in a circle. The teacher sits with us. He uses a student's desk. He puts his coat and

briefcase on the teacher's desk,
but he does not sit there.
There are posters of places in the
U.S. on all the walls my favorite
poster has a picture of a farm.
It reminds me of my uncle's
farm. There is a "No Smoking"
sign above the blackboard —
that's good!

In-Class Practice: About Your Class

1. Look at the people and things in your classroom. Make a list of
   everything you see:

   _____   _____   _____

   _____   _____   _____

   _____   _____   _____

2. Use the information on your list to describe your class on the next
   page. Then tear out the page and put it in your Writing Folder.

Describe Your Class

Name

Date

Tear out this page. Put it in your Writing Folder.

17

Meet Your Group

In-Class Practice: About You and Your Group

1. Fill out the information form in the box below. Give complete information.

Personal Information Form

---

1. Your name: _____

2. Your native
   country: _____

3. Your native
   language: _____

4. Your hobby,
   interest,
   or job: _____

5. Your field
   of study: _____

6. Other: _____

---

2. Now get into a group with two or three classmates. Read your information forms out loud to each other. You may ask each other for more information. Then write the information about you and your group members in the space below.

Group Information Form

Name: ___			
Country: ___			
Language: ___			
Hobby: ___			
Field: ___			
Other: ___			

Nicolas wrote this description of his group members:

There are 3 people in my group. Jan is from Poland. He speaks Polish and French. He lived with his cousin in France for 3 years. He went to high school there. Jan likes to ride his bicycle. He wants to ride across the U.S. Jan wants to study architecture. Patricia comes from Chile. She is 18. She speaks Spanish. She likes to sing, dance, and go to the movies. Patricia wants to be a musician. I am from Greece. I am 19. I speak Greek. I want to study business administration. I like to swim and play football. In the U.S. it's called soccer.

In-Class Practice: About Your Group

On the next page, write a description of the people in your group. Use the information about you and your group members on page 19. Then put the description in your Writing Folder.

Describe Your Group Members

Name _____

Date _____

_____

_____

_____

_____

_____

_____

_____

_____

_____

_____

_____

_____

_____

_____

_____

_____

_____

Introduce Yourself

At-Home Practice: About You

1. Read Patricia's personal information form:

Personal Information Form

1. Your name: *Patricia Gonzalez*

2. Your native country: *Chile*

3. Your native language: *Spanish*

4. Your hobby, interest, or job: *singing, dancing, walking, going to the movies, meeting people*

5. Your field of study: *Music*

6. Other: *favorite composer = Debussy*

---

2. Patricia read her personal information form to her group, and they asked more questions about her. At home, she wrote the following paragraph about herself:

My name is Patricia, and I come from Chile. My native language is Spanish. My hobbies are dancing, going for walks, reading and going to movies. I also love meeting people. My field of study is music. I play flute and piano. My favorite composer is Debussy.

3. Now write a paragraph about yourself. Start with the information on your personal information form. If you like, add more facts

from your group's discussion. Put this paragraph in your Writing Folder.

Write a Family Portrait

Fatema wanted to tell her classmates about her family. She drew her family tree and wrote about her family. Here is her family tree:

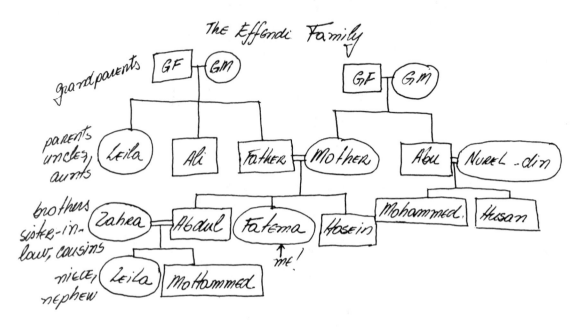

In her Academic Journal, Fatema wrote this about her family:

The Effendi ~~About My~~ Family
I have two brothers. My older brother Abdul studies in California. He is married and has two children. My little brother lives with my parents. He sends me a letter from home

every week. My father's brother, Ali, lives close to school. I live at his house.

Academic Journal Practice: Section 1

Draw your family tree. Then write about your family. If you prefer, write about a friend's family, or a famous family, or a make-believe family.

In-Class Practice: More Writing About Your Family

Bring your Academic Journal to class. Show a classmate your family tree and your entry about the family. Ask your classmate if he has any questions about the tree or about your entry. Write your classmate's questions here:

_____

_____

_____

_____

Answer your classmate's questions here:

_____

_____

_____

_____

Fatema read her family description to Patricia. Patricia asked Fatema these questions:

—Where do your parents live?
—What does your brother Abdul study?
—How old are your niece and nephew?

Fatema answered Patricia's questions. Then she rewrote her family description and added her answers. Where did she add the answers?

The Effendi Family

I have two brothers. My older brother Abdul studies chemistry in California. He is married and has two children. They are Leila, 2 years, and Mohammed, 8 months, My little brother lives with my parents in Cairo. He sends me a letter from home every week. My father's brother, Ali, lives close to school. I live at his house.

At-Home Practice: Rewriting the Family Story

1. Reread your answers to your classmate's questions on page 25.
2. Now rewrite the family story and add your answers. Put this paper in your Writing Folder.

More Writing on "My Own Topic"

In your Academic Journal you first made a list of topics to write about. Then you chose one topic and made a second list (Academic Journal Practice, p. 10). Here again is Maria's second list:

1- They dress very informally
2- the professors don't mind
3- In my country students dress formally

Maria chose number one, "They dress informally." She wrote this about her idea:

American students dress informally. In hot weather they wear shorts to class. Sometimes they don't wear shoes. In cold weather they wear jeans and sweaters, they don't dress up for parties. Everybody wears jeans and sneakers.

Turn to "My Own Topic" in your Academic Journal. Now look at your second list. Choose one idea from that list. Write about that idea. In the next chapter you will write more about your own topic.

Language Tale 2

Jan wanted to buy a bicycle. He looked in the telephone book and found Mike's Bike Shop, at 1403 Main Street. He called Mike to get directions to the store. Mike said, "It's on the corner of 13th and Main." But Jan *heard*, "It's on the corner of *30th* and Main." Jan took the bus to 30th and Main. He saw a grocery store, a record shop, a bank, and a barber shop, but no bike shop. A few minutes later Jan got on the bus and went home.

Why did Jan go home? Did you ever have a similar experience? What did *you* do? Tell the class.

Writing Folder

Fill out Progress Chart 1 on page 29 and put it in your Writing Folder. In your Writing Folder there should be:

1. Writing Questionnaire 1
2. Description of your class
3. Description of your group
4. The family paper
5. Progress Chart 1

Give the folder to your teacher. He will read everything in your folder to learn more about you and your writing. Then he will return your folder to you.

Summary

In this chapter you wrote about your class, yourself, and your own or someone else's family. You shared your writing with other students and you started a Writing Folder. You gave your folder to the teacher. You will continue to add papers to your Writing Folder in the next chapters.

Progress Chart 1:
Academic Journal Writing

Name

Date

Look at all the entries in your Academic Journal. Fill in the chart below. Tear out this page. Put it in your Writing Folder.

I used my Academic Journal for:

How many times?

	0	1	2	3	4	5+
Asking questions						
Answering questions						
Jotting down ideas						
Listing new words						
Writing about learning						
Taking notes						
Thinking on paper						
Other						

UNIT TWO

Developing Writing Strategies

In the next five chapters you will do many different kinds of writing: freewriting, draft writing, revising, and editing. In Chapter 7, you and your classmates will put together a magazine of some of your writing. Chapters 3 through 6 will prepare you to put this magazine together. You will also learn strategies to help you to start writing, continue writing, and finish writing.

CHAPTER 3

First Impressions

In this chapter

—You will do freewriting. Freewriting is a strategy for starting to write. It is thinking on paper.

—You will write two first drafts. Writing a first draft is a way to develop ideas you wrote down in freewriting and list making.

Read About First Impressions

Living in a foreign country can be fun and exciting. It can also be frustrating at times. The stories in this chapter are by international students at U.S. colleges and universities. The stories are about the students' early experiences in the United States. They are all final drafts.

Claire

It is always hard to start a new way of life. I came to the U.S. when I was seventeen years old and I went to an American high school for one year. I knew it would be very hard for me to study in English, but I had no choice. Going to an American high school was exciting, but also very difficult. Everything was so strange to me. In the beginning I couldn't understand what my teachers said. I even got lost trying to find my classes. I used to carry a dictionary with me all the time. My classmates always watched me while I looked up words in the dictionary. The words were so easy for them, but they were new to me. I felt so embarrassed! I still used my dictionary, though, because I wanted to learn new words. That year I learned two things: Pursue your goals. Don't worry about other people's opinions.

Ling

About one week after I came to the U.S. I went to the post office. There were many people there, so I had to wait in a long line. I waited and practiced saying in my mind, "I would like to send this package, please. And how much are air mail stamps?" But my turn came and I became nervous. I couldn't say anything. I just gave the clerk the package and answered her questions with "yes" or "no." Then she said, "That will be $3.13." When I gave her a $5 bill she asked, "Don't you have 13¢?" I answered, "Yes," and waited. In Chinese this positive reply means, "You are right. I don't have 13¢." But how could I expect an American to know this? The clerk thought I meant, "Yes, I have 13¢." Because of this misunderstanding we both waited for each other. She waited for the 13¢; I waited for my change. And the people behind me waited for both of us.

Nicolas

It was the day after I arrived in the U.S. I took a walk around the campus and then I walked to town. I was waiting on a street corner for the light to change. A young man came up to me and said something to me in English. I knew he was a foreigner. I shook my head and told him, "I do not understand." The young man just repeated the same thing, but slower this time. I still didn't understand. The stranger then showed me a map and pointed to "Kennedy Boulevard." Suddenly I understood. He wanted to know how to get to Kennedy Boulevard. I didn't know where it was. I wanted to help the young man anyway. I took the map from him and found Kennedy Boulevard. But I didn't know how to explain the directions to him. So I walked with him there. The next day was the first day of school. I went to my English class and sat down. There was the same young man! He was a student, just like me. Now we're friends.

Academic Journal Practice: Section 1

1. You read three stories about early experiences in the United States. Which story do you like best? Why? Write your answer in your Academic Journal.

2. Try to remember some of your early experiences in the United States. Make a list of them. For example, here is Ling's list:

The first time I ate popcorn

When I registered for school

The first time I went to the post office by myself

at the school cafeteria

Freewrite

Freewriting

Freewriting is one way to start writing.

Freewriting is writing you do for yourself.

Freewriting is writing nonstop, usually for ten to fifteen minutes.

How to freewrite: Start writing on a topic and don't stop until your time is up. Don't worry about grammar, punctuation, or spelling. Don't worry about the order of ideas. If you can't think of a word, leave a blank space.

Ling chose to write about "the first time I went to the post office by myself." Here is her freewriting:

The first time I went to the post office by myself

I am so nervous. It all started when I practice

my sentences. Say them over and over in my

mind. When I come to the post office lady (?)
I give her the package and can't speak. Answer
questions with yes or no. Then she says me
don't you have coins. Yes I say. The other
people on line get angry. english has its own way
to answer questions.

In-Class Practice: Freewriting

Choose an experience from your list of early experiences. In the space
below and on the next page, freewrite about your experience for fifteen
minutes. Like Ling, start with the words you wrote in your journal.

Freewrite about your experience for fifteen minutes.

_____

_____

_____

_____

_____

_____

_____

_____

_____

_____

_____

_____

_____

_____

_____

_____

_____

_____

_____

_____

Academic Journal Practice: Section 1

In your journal, write about your freewriting. Was it easy? Was it hard? Why? Did you like freewriting? Why or why not?

Give your Academic Journal to your teacher. She will read it, make comments, and return the journal to you.

Write a Draft About First Impressions

From Freewriting to a First Draft

You do freewriting for yourself. Only you read your freewriting.

A first draft is more complete than freewriting. Someone else can read a first draft. In a first draft you pay attention to the order of your ideas. You pay attention to grammar and punctuation. But a first draft is not perfect. Usually, it needs more work.

How do you use your freewriting to write a first draft? First, reread your freewriting. Then answer these questions about it:

What is my freewriting about?

What parts do I like?

What parts do I want to keep?

What parts do I want to take out?

What do I need to add?

The answers to these questions will help you write your first draft.

Reread Ling's freewriting about her experience at the post office. Ling's first draft is below. Her final draft is at the beginning of the chapter.

I went to the post office by myself. There were many people there, so I had to wait in a long line. I waited and practiced sentences. My turn came and I became nervous. I couldn't say anything. The clerk said to me, don't you have any coins? Yes, I said. According to Chinese language, this positive reply means, you are right, I don't have coins. How could I expect Americans to know this? Because of her misunderstanding we both waited for each other. The people in line waited for both of us.

In-Class Practice: Note the Differences

What differences between Ling's freewriting and first draft do you see? What did Ling add to her first draft? What did she take out? Write your answers below and on the next page.

What differences between Ling's freewriting and first draft do you see?

_____

_____

_____

_____

_____

_____

_____

_____

_____

_____

_____

_____

_____

_____

_____

_____

At-Home Practice: From Freewriting to a First Draft

Write a first draft about your experience. Use your freewriting as a starting point. The advice in the box "From Freewriting to a First Draft" will help you use your freewriting to write a first draft. Bring your draft to class.

In-Class Practice: Reading and Commenting

1. Read your first draft to another student in the class. Next listen to your partner's first draft. Then write comments about your partner's draft on Response Sheet A on the next page. (For an example of answers to Response Sheet A, see Chapter 5.)

2. Tear out the response sheets and exchange them. Read your partner's comments. Make sure you understand them.

3. Give your draft and Response Sheet A to your teacher. Your teacher will write comments on your draft. She will tell you her favorite parts, the parts she doesn't understand, and the parts

Response Sheet A: "First Impressions"

Writer _____

Partner _____

Date _____

1. My partner's first draft is about:

2. I remember these words:

3. My favorite part is:

4. I don't understand:

5. I want to know more about:

6. Other comments:

Tear out this page. Give it to your partner.

she wants to know more about. She will return your draft and Response Sheet A to you. Then put your draft and Response Sheet A in your Writing Folder. In Chapter 5 you will write another draft of this paper.

More Writing on "My Own Topic"

Here is Maria's topic and list of ideas again:

The way American students dress
1- They dress very informally.
2- the professors don't mind
3- In my country students dress formally.

She wrote this draft about all the ideas on her list:

American students dress informally. In hot weather they wear shorts to class. Sometimes they don't wear shoes. In cold weather they wear jeans and sweaters. they don't dress up for parties. Everybody wears jeans and sneakers. In my country students dress formally. Girls usually wear dresses or skirts and blouses. Boys wear slacks and shirts. Boys sometimes wear jackets and ties to parties. American professors don't mind when students come to class in shorts. The professors in my country want students to dress nicely. In my country students dress nicely to show respect for the professors.

Turn to "My Own Topic" in your Academic Journal. In Chapter 2 you chose one idea from your list and wrote about it. Now write a draft about the other ideas on the list. (Don't worry about the order of ideas. You will work on that later.)

In-Class Practice: Vocabulary Exercise B

1. Each student chooses one or two new words from her Academic Journal and tells them to the teacher. The teacher writes the words on the board. Which words do you know? What do they mean? Tell the class. The teacher will write the definitions on the board.

2. Copy the words from the board onto the Vocabulary Exercise Chart. Copy the definitions, too.

Vocabulary Exercise Chart B

Word   *Definitions*

_____   _____

                       _____

                       _____

                       _____

_____   _____

                       _____

                       _____

                       _____

_____   _____

                       _____

                       _____

_____   _____

                       _____

                       _____

_____   _____

_____   _____

                       _____

                       _____

                       _____

_____   _____

                       _____

                       _____

                       _____

Academic Journal Practice: Section 2

Copy Vocabulary Exercise Chart B into the vocabulary section of your Academic Journal.

Summary

In this chapter you did some freewriting. You wrote two first drafts, "First Impressions" and "My Own Topic." You read your "First Impressions" draft to another student and you got some comments. You gave the "First Impressions" draft to your teacher and you got more comments. In the next chapters you will do some more freewriting, draft writing, commenting, and rewriting.

CHAPTER 4

Observations

In this chapter

—You will write observations. Observation is looking at things and thinking about them. Scientists use observation in the laboratory. Businesspeople use it in the marketplace. Observation is a research technique.

—You will start to use Section 3 of your Academic Journal. This section is for taking research notes and other kinds of notes.

Observe a Place

Maria went to her school cafeteria on the first day of class. She observed carefully. Here is her first draft about her experience:

I went with another student, and we didn't know what to do. we stood in line and watched the students in front of us. they got their food and they went to the cashier, so we did this too. I didn't understand the cashier.

I look at her machine and saw "9.38". So I gave her $9.50 and got some change back. We found an empty table, and then we ate. It was noisy. We didn't talk much. My friend ask "Do we just leave our trays on the table?" We looked around at the others students. They took their dirty trays to a counter, so we did this too. I still don't know everything about the cafeteria, but I'm less afraid to go there now. It's not so bad.

In-Class Practice: Freewriting and Discussion

What does Maria's story make you think of? Freewrite your ideas below (ten minutes). Then share your ideas with the class.

Maria's story made me think of _____

_____

_____

_____

_____

_____

_____

_____

_____

Take Observation Notes

Observers sometimes take notes to remember everything. Chung got an assignment to go to a place, observe for thirty minutes, and write a description. He went to a coffee shop. Here are his notes:

Date: Oct 3, Friday   Time: 12:30 p.m (lunch)

# of people: 23 customers, 3 waitresses (1 behind counter, 2 at tables)

# of tables: 12.

Slow service, but no one is angry or impatient. Coffee comes quickly. Mostly girls, but one boy and girl at table in back & a boy alone in back. Waitresses are all older women. They are like American mothers. My sandwich comes in 12 — 1/2 minutes. Food is ok. People at counter don't talk to each other —— don't look at each other —— they look at their food, or at wall in front of them. I ordered ham sandwich & it's ok. I also got pickle (very bad) a tiny paper cup of very sweet salad. Why did I get these —— I didn't ask for them.

12:53 — Some of the people are leaving. I asked for my bill. About 17 people (customers) here now — they are still eating. 3 girls leave together — on table, ashtray is really full & there are 3 cups. They only had coffee. Maybe they talked about their boyfriends — they were laughing very loud. Dark room, chairs have red seats — soft plastic, waitresses all wear yellow dresses, windows on one wall. I'm ready to leave — who is still here? boy at back — he was here at 12:30 — he is still reading a book & eating a bowl of soup. I leave my table at exactly 1:12.

In-Class Practice: Choosing a Place to Observe

1. Here is a list of places to observe. These places are at or near your school. What can you add to the list?

Admissions office	Dormitory
Language lab	Cafeteria/local coffee shop
Library	Hallway in front of class
Bookstore	Computer center
Student union/lounge	Photocopy center

Other _____   _____

_____   _____

_____   _____

_____   _____

_____   _____

2. As a class, choose the place each student will observe. What place

will you observe? Write it here: _____

Now you will start to use Section 3 of your Academic Journal. This section is for taking notes. Students take notes:

—When they read
—When they listen to lectures
—When they do research
—When they study for exams

Academic Journal Practice: Section 3

Go to the place you chose to observe. Spend about fifteen to thirty minutes observing. Take observation notes in your Academic Journal.

Share and Respond

Sharing

Sharing is reading your writing aloud to others. Sharing helps you hear your writing in a new way.

Sharing may help you hear differences between what you *thought* you wrote and what appears on your paper.

How to share: Read your writing to others. You can read to friends, to classmates, or to your teacher. Always read your writing twice.

Responding

Responding is commenting about someone else's writing. When you respond, you tell the writer what his writing communicated.

How to respond: There are many ways to respond to someone else's writing. You can write your response or you can say it.

Do you have questions? Ask the writer.

What do you like? Tell the writer.

What do you remember? Tell the writer.

What don't you understand? Tell the writer.

In-Class Practice: Sharing and Responding

1. Share: Meet with two of your classmates. Share your observation notes with each other once.
2. Respond: Follow these steps.
   a. Each group member shares his observation notes again with the group.
   b. The other group members write their comments on Response Sheet B on page 51. (For an example of answers to Response Sheet B, see Chapter 5.)
   c. Then the other group members give the response sheets to the writer.

Repeat these steps for each group member.

Write a Draft from Observation Notes

Chung used his observation notes to write this description of the coffee shop. This description is a first draft.

The coffee shop on the corner of 8th and Vine is not very big. The place has windows along one wall (north) and is very dark. It has only twelve tables and a counter. Each table has two chairs, and there are six high chairs at the counter. The chairs at the tables have red plastic seats. At lunchtime on Friday, it was very busy. Only three waitresses were serving about twenty-three people. The waitresses were pleasant, but the service was slow. Some people were sitting alone. They were reading books or newspapers. I didn't see very many boys. I think that mostly girls go to this coffee shop.

In-Class Practice: Note the Differences

How is Chung's description of the coffee shop different from his observation notes? Below, list the differences you see. Then discuss your list with the class.

_____

_____

_____

_____

Response Sheet B: "Observation"

Writer

Responder

Date

1. Place observed:

2. What did the writer tell me about this place?

3. What other things do I want to know about this place?

4. Give this response sheet to the writer.

Response Sheet B: "Observation"

Writer

Responder

Date

1. Place observed:

2. What did the writer tell me about this place?

3. What other things do I want to know about this place?

4. Give this response sheet to the writer.

Chung explained to his class how he used his observation notes to write his first draft. Read Chung's explanation. Then discuss it with your classmates.

Chung: First I typed my notes. Then I read them two times. I circled the parts about the *place*. Then I put a box around the parts about *people*.

Date: Oct 3, Friday   Time: 12:30 p.m. (lunch)

# of people: 23 customers, 3 waitresses (1 behind counter, 2 at tables) # of tables: 12

slow service, but no one is angry or impatient. Coffee comes quickly. Mostly girls, but one boy & girl at table in back & a boy alone in back. Waitresses are all older women. They are like American mothers. My sandwich comes in 12½ minutes. Food is ok. People at counter don't talk to each other -- don't look at each other -- they look at their food, or at wall in front of them. I ordered ham sandwich & it's ok. I also got pickle (very bad) & tiny paper cup of very sweet salad. Why did I get these--I didn't ask for them. 12:53--some of the people are leaving. I asked for my bill. About 17 people (customers) here now -- they are still eating. 3 girls leave together--on table, ashtray is really full & there are 3 cups. They only had coffee. Maybe they talked about their boyfriends--they were laughing very loud. Dark room, chairs have red seats--soft plastic, waitresses all wear yellow dresses, windows on one wall. I'm ready to leave--who is still here? Boy at back--he was here at 12:30--he is still reading a book & eating a bowl of soup. I leave my table at exactly 1:12.

Chung: Then I copied all these parts onto another sheet of paper. I put the place things in one column and the people things in another. I reread the lists and I checked the things to put in my first draft. Then I crossed out everything else.

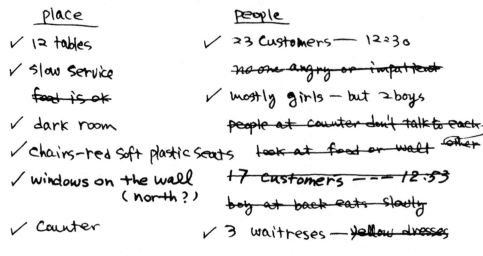

place

✓ 12 tables

✓ slow service

~~food is ok~~

✓ dark room

✓ chairs—red soft plastic seats

✓ windows on the wall
     (north ?)

✓ Counter

people

✓ 23 Customers — 12:30

~~no one angry or impatient~~

✓ mostly girls — but 2 boys

~~people at counter don't talk to each other~~

~~look at food or wall~~

17 customers — — — 12:53

~~boy at back eats slowly~~

✓ 3 waitreses — ~~yellow dresses~~

Chung: Then I decided to describe the place first and the people second. And then I wrote my first draft.

Now reread Chung's first draft on page 49.

From Observation Notes to a First Draft

You take observation notes to remember everything you saw. Notes are not organized. They may not be complete sentences.

In a first draft you add information to help the reader understand. In a first draft you pay attention to the order of your ideas. You pay attention to grammar and punctuation. But a first draft is not perfect. Usually, it needs more work.

How do you use your observation notes to write a first draft? First, reread your notes. Then answer these questions about them:

    Who will be my readers?

    What information do I want to add for my readers?

    What information do I want to take out?

    What do I want to put first, next, after that, and so on?

The answers to these questions will help you write your first draft.

At-Home Practice: From Observation Notes to a First Draft

Use your observation notes and the advice in the box above to write a first draft. Use your classmates' responses (Response Sheet B) to decide what information to add. Put your draft in your Writing Folder.

Fill out Progress Chart 2 on page 57. Put it in your Writing Folder. Then give your folder to your teacher. Your teacher will read your draft ("Observation" paper). He will comment on your ideas and on their organization. He will also read Progress Chart 2.

Summary

In this chapter you took observation notes. You shared these notes with other students. You received and gave responses. Then you wrote a first draft. In the next chapter you will work more on your "First Impressions" draft and your "Observation" draft.

Progress Chart 2: Developing a First Draft

Name

Date

Was it easy? Difficult? Why?

1. Freewriting

1. _____
   _____
   _____

2. Taking observa-
   tion notes

2. _____
   _____
   _____

3. Writing a first
   draft

3. _____
   _____
   _____

4. Sharing

4. _____
   _____
   _____

5. Responding

5. _____
   _____
   _____

What did you write in your Academic Journal?

	Yes	No
Ideas		
Questions		
New words		
Notes		
Other		

Tear out this page. Put it in your Writing Folder.   **57**

CHAPTER 5

Revising

In this chapter

—You will learn to revise your first drafts. Revising is a strategy for continuing to write. All good writers use it. Revising is not easy, but it is a good strategy to know. There are many ways to revise.

In Chapter 3 you wrote a first draft about an experience ("First Impressions") and a first draft of "My Own Topic." In Chapter 4 you wrote a first draft of an observation. In this chapter you will revise these drafts. Then, in Chapter 7, you will edit these drafts and put them into a magazine for your classmates.

Revising

Revising is changing your writing. Sometimes, you get response from a classmate or teacher, and then you make changes. Other times, you reread your writing alone, and then you make changes. Why do you make changes? Because you want to make your writing understandable and more interesting. You might change an idea, a paragraph, a sentence, or a phrase. You might decide to reorganize, add something, or take something out. Revising will help you communicate your ideas more clearly.

Read About One Revision Process

Ling wanted to publish her "First Impressions" story in the class magazine. First she needed to revise her story to make it clearer for her readers. Below, Ling explains her steps for revising—her revising process. Read her explanation and look at her revisions.

Ling: I read my first draft to Jan.

Ling's First Draft

I went to the post office by myself. There were many people there, so I had to wait in a long line. I waited and practiced sentences. My turn came and I became nervous. I couldn't say anything. The clerk said to me, don't you have any coins? Yes, I said. According to Chinese language, this positive reply means, you are right, I don't have coins. How could I expect Americans to know this? Because of her misunderstanding we both waited for each other. The people in line waited for both of us.

Ling: Jan liked the story. He filled out the response sheet and gave it to me.

Jan's Response Sheet

Writer   *Ling*

Partner   *Jan*

1. My partner's first draft is about: *a visit to the post office*

2. I remember these words: *coins, people in line, nervous, practiced sentences*

3. My favorite part is: *You were nervous (I'm always nervous too.)*

4. I don't understand: *I don't understand the Chinese language rule.*

5. I want to know more about: *What were you sending? Is this first time in post office?*

6. Other comments: *What did you & the clerk say?*

Read Ling's explanation in response to Jan and look at her revisions.

Ling: At home I reread Jan's response. Then I cooked dinner and did my math homework. Finally, I started to revise. First, I typed my first draft. Jan asked, "What did you and the clerk say?" So I added more dialogue. In the dialogue I put "13¢" for "coins." That's more specific. Jan asked, "What were you sending?" So I also added, "I would like to send this package, please. And how much are airmail stamps?" Next I changed the first sentence. I want people to know that I was a new

Ling's First Draft, with Revisions

About one week after I came to the US

∧ I went to the post office. ~~by~~

~~myself.~~ There were many people

there, so I had to wait in a long

line. I waited and practiced ∧
saying in my mind, "I would like to send this
package, please. And how much are airmail stamps?"
~~sentences.~~ My turn came and I
∧

became nervous. I couldn't say
"That will be $3.13." I gave her a $5 bill,
and she asked,
anything. The clerk said to me, ∧
13¢?"

"Don't you have ~~any coins? Yes,~~
I answered, "yes," and waited
~~I said.~~ According to Chinese

person in this country. This
will help them understand
why I was nervous.

language, this positive reply

y
means, you are right. I don't have

13¢."
~~coins~~. How could I expect

Americans to know this? Because

of her misunderstanding, we both

waited for each other. The people

in line waited for both of us.

In-Class Practice: Write and Discuss

How did Ling use Jan's responses to revise her first draft? What comments did she use? How? What comments did she not use? Write your answers below. Then discuss them with the class.

_____

_____

_____

_____

_____

_____

_____

Drafts

Drafts are different versions of a paper.

Each time you revise a draft and make a clean copy you have another draft.

    draft 1 + revisions → clean copy = draft 2

    draft 2 + revisions → clean copy = draft 3

    draft 3 + revisions → clean copy = draft 4

    . . . and so on.

When you stop revising, you have a final draft. You edit final drafts.

Next, Ling explains her steps for revising her second draft.

Ling: I made a lot of revisions in my first draft. It was hard to read, so I retyped it. I read this second draft, and I saw a problem. I didn't explain the misunderstanding about the Chinese language rule. And *"her* misunderstanding" isn't nice. I misunderstood, too. So I changed the last three sentences. Maybe Jan will understand the Chinese language rule now. Then I reread to look for mistakes. I changed "According to Chinese language" to "In Chinese." I think that's better. Then I typed it again, very carefully.

Ling's Second Draft, with Revisions

About one week after I came to

the U.S. I went to the post office.

There were many people there, so

I had to wait in a long line. I

waited and practiced saying in

my mind, "I would like to send

this package, please. And how

much are airmail stamps?"∧ ~~My~~ *But*

turn came and I became nervous.

I couldn't say anything.∧ *I just* ~~The clerk~~
gave the clerk the package and answered her
questions with "yes" or "no." Then she said,
~~said to me~~∧ "That will be $3.13." *When*

I gave her a $5 bill ~~and~~ she

asked, "Don't you have 13¢?" I

answered, "Yes," and waited.

~~According to~~ *In* Chinese ~~language~~,

this positive reply means, "You

are right. I don't have 13¢."∧ ~~How~~ *But*

could I expect∧ *an* American∕ to
The clerk thought I meant,
"Yes. I have 13¢."
know this?∧ Because of ~~her~~ *this*

misunderstanding, we both
she waited for the 13¢; I waited for my
change.
waited for each other.∧ The people
behind me
~~in line~~ waited for both of us.
∧

In-Class Practice: Revising Strategies

Reread Ling's explanations of her revising process. How many times did she use the following revising strategies? Share your answers with the class.

Strategy	How Many Times?
Rereading	_____
Adding	_____
Replacing	_____
Taking out	_____
Typing a new draft	_____
Waiting	_____

Revise "First Impressions" Draft

At-Home Practice: Revising the First Draft of Your "First Impressions" Paper

1. Reread your first draft. Reread Response Sheet A from your partner. Read your teacher's response to your first draft. (Your first draft and the responses are in your Writing Folder.)
2. Think about these questions:
   —Are the responses from your partner and from your teacher different? How? Are the responses the same? How?
   —What will you add to your first draft?
   —What will you take out?
   —What will you replace?
3. Revise your first draft. Put the first draft, Response Sheet A, teacher's response, and the new draft in your Writing Folder. You will edit your new draft in Chapter 7.

Academic Journal Practice: Section 1

Which strategies did you use to revise your "First Impressions" draft? List them in your Academic Journal.

Study Another Revision Process

People revise differently. For example, Ling's revising process is not the same as Maria's revising process. Maria revised her description of the cafeteria. Here is Maria's first draft again:

> I went with another student, and we didn't know what to do. We stood in line and watched the students in front of us. They got their food and they went to the cashier, so we did this too. I didn't understand the cashier.
>
> I look at her machine and saw "2.38". So I gave her $2.50 and got some change back. We found an empty table, and then we ate. It was noisy. We didn't talk much. My friend ask "Do we just leave our trays on the table?" We looked around at the others students. They took their dirty trays to a counter, so we did this too. I still don't know everything about the cafeteria, but I'm less afraid to go there now. It's not so bad.

Maria shared her first draft with Fatema and Nicolas. Their response sheets are on the following page.

Response Sheet B: "Observation"

Writer *Maria*

Responder *Fatema*

Date

1. Place observed: *cafeteria*

2. What did the writer tell me about this place?

   She didn't know what to do. She watched other students. dirty trays go to a counter.

3. What other things do I want to know about this place?

   crowded? what does it look like? windows? Do teachers eat there?

4. Give this response sheet to the writer.

Response Sheet B: "Observation"

Writer *Maria*

Responder *Nicolas*

Date

1. Place observed: *school cafeteria*

2. What did the writer tell me about this place?

   went with a friend. Watching to learn what to do. After eating, students take trays to a special place.

3. What other things do I want to know about this place?

   How was the food? Big choice? Do they give you a lot?

4. Give this response sheet to the writer.

Maria wanted to revise. She met again with Fatema and Nicolas. The three students talked about Maria's first draft:

Maria: Your response sheets were good, but I need more help. I want to revise this draft.

Fatema: What do you want to do?

Maria: I think . . .

Nicolas: I know! You can add more description.

Fatema: Yes. What color are the walls?

Maria: No. Not a description. I don't like that.

Nicolas: What do you like?

Maria: I like. . . . I want to say to other students, "Do this, and do this, and you will be OK."

Fatema: I don't understand.

Nicolas: You want to, um, what is . . . you want to explain?

Maria: Yes. The cafeteria is different. It's very different for foreign students. I want to tell foreign students, "It's ok. It's easy. Don't be afraid."

Fatema: Give advice? You want to give advice?

Maria: Yes. I want to give advice.

Nicolas: That's good. That's a good idea.

This talk helped Maria. She decided to write advice to foreign students. She decided to tell them how to use the cafeteria. She reread her first draft and Fatema's and Nicolas's response sheets. Then she wrote a second draft:

The student cafeteria is a new experience for foreign students. There is much food, and it's a big place with no windows. It's very busy at lunch. People stand in line. People behind you say, "Hurry up! I'm hungry!" People in front of you say "Give me more meatloaf please". Everything happens very fast. What do you eat? where do you sit? How much does it cost?

what is "meatloaf?" Remember this advice:

1. watch other people and do what they do.
2. Don't go alone.

In-Class Practice: Note the Differences

Reread Maria's first and second drafts. Reread the response sheets and the discussion earlier in this chapter. How did Maria use the response sheets to revise? How did she use the discussion with Fatema and Nicolas to revise? Write your answers and discuss them with the class.

_____

_____

_____

_____

Maria gave her first and second drafts and the response sheets to her teacher. The teacher read everything. Then she wrote this response to Maria:

Maria - The cafeteria sounds very confusing. You give some good advice to help others. But I still have some questions. Why do you say "Don't go alone"? And you say "Watch other people and do what they do." People do different things. Who should I watch?

Maria read her teacher's response, and then she revised again. Here is her final draft:

The student cafeteria at our school is a new experience for foreign students. There is much food, and it is a big place with no windows. You stand in line to buy lunch. People behind you say "Hurry up I'm hungry!" People in front of you say, "Give me more meatloaf, please" Everything happens very fast. what do you eat? where do you sit? How much does it cost? what is "meatloaf"?

Remember this advice: 1 How do you know what to do? watch other people and do what the majority does. 2 Don't go alone. With a friend, you won't be afraid. 3 Don't be afraid to ask for help.

Academic Journal Practice: Section 1

Look at Maria's second and final drafts. What did she take out of her second draft? What did she keep? What new information did she add? How did she use her teacher's response to revise?

In-Class Practice: Talking About Revising

Reread Response Sheet B from your partners. Meet again with your partners. Share the first drafts of your observation papers again. Talk about how to revise. To begin your discussion, ask each writer, "What do you want to do to revise your draft?"

Revise "Observation" Draft

At-Home Practice: Revising the First Draft of Your "Observation" Paper

1. Reread Response Sheet B from your partners. Read your teacher's response to your first draft.

2. Think about these questions:

   —Are the responses from your partners and from your teacher different? How? Are the responses the same? How?

—What will you add to your first draft?

—What will you take out?

—What will you replace?

3. Revise your first draft. Put the first draft, response sheets, teacher's response, and new draft in your Writing Folder. (You will edit your new draft in Chapter 7.)

4. Fill out Progress Chart 3. Put it in your Writing Folder.

More Writing on "My Own Topic"

In Chapter 3 you wrote a first draft of "My Own Topic" in your Academic Journal. Copy this draft from your Academic Journal onto a sheet of paper. Bring your first draft to class. Get together with two other students. Share your first drafts and then respond. Tell the writer:

1. What you remember

2. What you like

3. What you want to know more about

Fill out Response Sheet C on page 73. This response sheet will help you remember your group's responses. Put your first draft and Response Sheet C in your Writing Folder. You will revise your first draft in Chapter 6.

Give your Writing Folder to your teacher. She will read the second drafts of your "First Impressions" paper and observation paper. She will also read Progress Chart 3. Then she will return your folder to you.

Summary

In this chapter you read about and discussed two students' revising processes. You used student and teacher responses to revise two first drafts: "First Impressions" and "Observation." You also wrote about your own revising process. In the next chapter you will write about your field of study.

Progress Chart 3: Revising a Draft

Name

Date

Reread the first draft of your "Observation" paper. Reread the next draft.
What changes did you make? Fill in the chart below. Then tear out this
page. Put it in your Writing Folder.

1. I added   1. _____

   _____

   _____

   _____

2. I took out   2. _____

   _____

   _____

   _____

3. I replaced   3. _____

   _____

   _____

   _____

How did you use your partners' and teacher's responses to revise?

Response Sheet C: "My Own Topic"

Name

Date

My group members:

My group remembered:

My group liked:

My group wanted to know more about:

Other comments:

CHAPTER 6

Research

In this chapter

—You will do some research and write a report about your field of study. You will begin with what you know about your field, write some research questions, and try to answer those questions. Research is an important part of academic and professional life.

Fields of Study

In 1982–83, most foreign students in the United States studied in the following fields:

Fields of Study	Number of Foreign Students
Engineering	77,990
Business and management	60,960
Physical/life sciences	26,830
Math/computer sciences	25,680
Social sciences	23,910
Fine/applied arts	15,510

Education	12,260
Humanities	11,990
Health sciences	11,970
Agriculture	8,540

Academic Journal Practice: Section 1

Read the chart. Where do you fit in? Why is engineering the most popular field for foreign students? Think of some reasons. Write down your comments or questions about the chart.

In-Class Practice: Fields-of-Study Survey

Find out the fields of study of all the students in your class. Fill in the chart below:

Fields-of-Study Survey

Fields of Study	*Number of Students in This Field*
_____	_____
_____	_____
_____	_____
_____	_____
_____	_____
_____	_____
_____	_____
_____	_____
_____	_____
_____	_____

Total students
in our class   _____

Read About One Field of Study

Patricia is a flutist; her field of study is music. She and Jan discussed the field. They discussed what they knew about it. Patricia had some questions about her field. She and Jan discussed these questions, too. Patricia filled in the chart below:

Music
_____
Name of field

I know

Jobs - Musicians can teach music

Musicians can play in orchestras or chamber groups.

Salary - Music teachers earn between $15 + 50 an hour for private lessons.

Education - You can major in music at a college or university. You can go to music school.

Future - it is very difficult to get an orchestra job!

I want to find out

What are other jobs for musicians?

What is the starting salary of an orchestra player?

What courses are required for music majors in colleges and universities?

Patricia looked for answers to her questions. She went to the music department of her college. She read the course catalogue. Then she spoke to the secretary of the music department. She took notes in her Academic Journal. Here is her entry:

3/15 I found out:
BA in music - 120 credits. Audition required.

Music Courses	Non-Music Courses
Music Theory	Natural science (6 credits)
Music History	Social Science (12 credits)
Ear Training	Foreign Language (6 credits)
Sight reading	Expository Writing (6 credits)

Performance
Private Study

The secretary of the music department was very friendly. She asked me, "How many years have you been playing the flute?" I answered, "Ten years -- since I was 8 years old." She said "You must be very good." I thought, "You are right, but I always get nervous at auditions." She gave me an appointment for next Wednesday at 3:00. I will meet with one of the music professors. Maybe he can answer my other questions.

Research Your Field of Study

In-Class Practice: Talking About Your Field of Study

Find two to five classmates in your field of study. Form a group. Talk about:

1. What you know about your field (jobs, salary, education, future)
2. What you want to find out

Fill in the chart below:

Name of Field   _____

We Know   *We Want to Find Out*

Jobs:

Salary:

Education:

Future:

In-Class Practice: Questions About Your Field of Study

1. Now write a list of questions your group has about your field. These are your research questions. If you need more room, write in your Academic Journal.

Research Questions About the Field

2. Here are some ways of finding information to answer your research questions. Each student in the group should choose *one* way of

finding information. Then each student should use his way of finding information to answer his research questions.

Ways of Finding Information

—Read college catalogue
—Ask librarian
—Talk to students in the field
—Go to career counseling
—Ask foreign student advisor

—Other _____

_____

What will be your way of finding information? _____

Academic Journal Practice: Section 3

Answer these questions:

1. What are the answers to your research questions?
2. How and where did you find these answers?

You can read Patricia's entry earlier in this chapter to give you some ideas.

Patricia found the answers to her questions about her field. Then she wrote this report:

To become a music major at American College, you must audition. You must play for 15 minutes. Music majors must take: Music Theory (12 credits), Music History (6 credits), ear training (12 credits), sight reading (12 credits), private study (24 credits), group performance (24 credits). You must also take 6 credits of natural science, 12 credits of social science, 6 credits of foreign language and 6 credits of expository writing.

Most music majors become music teachers. In the U.S. they receive certification to teach in public schools. Some get higher degrees to teach at colleges and universities. Some music majors become performers. They join orchestras and chamber groups. Orchestra members earn between $14,000 and $50,000 a year. Some have private students.

At-Home Practice: Writing a Research Report

Use the answers to your research questions to write a report about your field. Include information about jobs, salary, education, and future. The report will be a first draft.

In-Class Practice: Sharing and Responding

Read the first draft of your report to a student who is *not* in your field. Then your partner will read his draft to you. Fill out Response Sheet D on page 83 and give it to your partner.

Put the first draft of your research report and Response Sheet D in your Writing Folder. Give the folder to your teacher. He will read and respond to your first draft using the questions from Response Sheet D. Later in this chapter you will revise your research report.

In-Class Practice: Vocabulary Exercise C

Each student chooses one or two new words from his Academic Journal and tells them to the teacher. The teacher writes the words on the board. Which words do you know? What do they mean? Tell the class. The teacher will write the definitions on the board.

Copy the words from the board onto Vocabulary Exercise Chart C. Copy the definitions, too.

Vocabulary Exercise Chart C

Word   *Definitions*

_____   _____

                      _____

                      _____

_____   _____

                      _____

                      _____

_____   _____

                      _____

                      _____

_____   _____

                      _____

                      _____

_____   _____

                      _____

                      _____

_____   _____

                      _____

Academic Journal Practice: Section 2

Copy Vocabulary Exercise Chart C into the vocabulary section of your Academic Journal.

Response Sheet D:
Report on Field of Study

Writer

Responder

Date

1. What did you learn from your partner's report?

2. Did you understand everything? Please explain.

3. What other things do you want to know about the field?

Tear out this page. Give it to your partner.

Brainstorm

You already used list making and freewriting to start writing. Now you will use brainstorming to begin writing about a new topic.

At-Home Practice: *Choosing a New Topic*

Look through your Academic Journal. Find a topic to write about. You will use this topic for brainstorming.

Brainstorming

Brainstorming is a quick way to develop ideas for writing.

Brainstorming is a free exchange of ideas about a topic.

Brainstorming helps a writer decide what to write about a topic.

Here is an example of four students brainstorming. (See map of brainstorming session on p. 86.)

Hiro: I want to write about how machines keep people alive.

Claire: I read in the newspaper about a baby who will die without a life machine.

Fatema: Some old people need life machines, too.

Anatoly: Or people who were in accidents.

Claire: Do you want to write about babies, old people, or people who were in accidents?

Hiro: Just old people, I think.

Fatema: It is hard for the families of the old people. The machines are expensive. And the old people can't talk or think.

Anatoly: But they can't turn off the machine!

Claire: Who can't turn off the machine? The doctor? The family?

Hiro: Sometimes the family wants to turn off the machine. Then the government says no. I want to write about this.

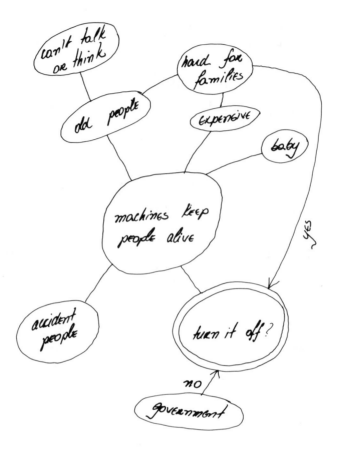

In-Class Practice: Brainstorming

1. Bring your new topic to class. Brainstorm with a small group of classmates. Ask each other these questions to start brainstorming:

   Why did you choose this topic?

   What interests you most about this topic?

   What is important about this topic?

   How will you begin your first draft?

2. Next fill in the chart on the following page. Then put the chart in your Writing Folder.

At-Home Practice: Writing a First Draft

Write a first draft about your new topic. Use the ideas you got from brainstorming. Put this first draft in your Writing Folder. You will revise this first draft in Chapter 8.

Brainstorming on My Topic

Name

Date

My topic _____

My group members _____

We said this about my topic: _____

_____

_____

_____

_____

_____

_____

_____

_____

_____

_____

_____

_____

_____

Tear out this page. Put it in your Writing Folder.

Revise the Research Report

At-Home Practice: Using the Responses to Revise

1. Reread Response Sheet D from your partner. Read your teacher's response.
2. Think about these questions:

   Are the responses from your partner and from your teacher different? How? Are the responses the same? How?

   What will you add to your first draft?

   What will you take out?

   What will you replace?
3. Revise your report.

Academic Journal Practice: Section 1

Reread the first and second drafts of your research report. What did you add? What did you take out? What did you keep?

   Give your Academic Journal to your teacher. Your teacher will write comments under some of the entries.

In-Class Practice: Sharing Second Drafts of Research Reports

Get back into your field-of-study group. Share your second drafts. Then choose one report from your group to present to the whole class. The writer of the chosen report will read it to the whole class.

In-Class Practice: Presenting Chosen Reports to the Class

1. Listen to the chosen report from each group. Write down one thing you learn from each report.
2. Discuss with the whole class what you learn from each report.
3. Put your own second draft in your Writing Folder.

Revising "My Own Topic"

Maria used her classmates' responses to revise the first draft of her paper about the way American students dress. Here is her second draft:

American students dress informally. In hot weather they wear shorts to class. Sometimes they don't wear shoes. In cold weather they wear jeans and sweaters.

Everybody wears jeans and sneakers. In my country most students dress formally. Women usually wear dresses or skirts and blouses to class. Men wear slacks and shirts. But some students in my country want to dress like American students. They wear jeans, T-shirts and sneakers to class. American professors don't mind when students come to class in shorts. The professors in my country want students to dress nicely. In my country students dress nicely to show respect for the professors.

She gave her second draft to her teacher. Her teacher commented on this draft and returned it to her. Here are his comments:

Maria — You say, "American students dress informally." You also say, "In my country, students dress nicely to show respect for the professors." Do you mean that American students don't respect their professors?

Read Maria's second draft. Read her teacher's comments. How will Maria use her teacher's comments to revise? What do you think? Discuss your ideas with the class.

Use Response Sheet C to revise the first draft of your own topic. Then give your second draft and Response Sheet C to your teacher. Your teacher will give you more response. In the next chapter you will write a final draft of your paper.

Summary

In this chapter you did some research about your field of study. You discussed your field with other students. You made up research questions. Then you tried to find answers to your questions. You wrote the first draft of a report about your field. You used student and teacher responses to revise that report. You also did some brainstorming and you wrote a first draft. In the next chapter you will edit three drafts: your "Field-of-Study" report, your "Observation" paper, and your "First Impressions" paper.

CHAPTER 7

Editing

In this chapter

— You will edit your final drafts by yourself and with the help of other students. You will also help other students edit their final drafts. Editing is working on the punctuation, spelling, and grammar of final drafts. All writers get help from editors to correct their writing.

— You will make the class magazine.

Editing

Editing is the last step in writing.

Editing is polishing your writing to make it easy to read.

Editing is finding and correcting the grammar, punctuation, and spelling mistakes in a final draft.

How to edit: Read your final draft a few times. Mark and correct any mistakes you see. Then show your final draft to a friend, classmate, or teacher. That person will look for other mistakes. Then correct these mistakes. Use an English/English dictionary and a grammar handbook.

Learn Editing Marks

Nicolas read his final draft. He found some mistakes, and he marked and corrected them. Then he met with Hiro. Hiro found some more mistakes, and he marked them. Later Nicolas and Hiro corrected these mistakes. Here is Nicolas's final draft with the editing marks:

line 1   It was day after I arrived in US. I took a walk around the

2   campos and then I walked to town. I was waiting at the

3   street corner for the light to be change. A young man came

4   up to me and say something to me in english. I knew he

5   is foreigner. I shook my head and told him I do not

6   understand. The young man just repeated same thing but

7   slower this time. I still didnt understand. The stranger then

8   show me a map and point to the Kennedy Boulevard.

9   Suddenly I understood. He wanted to know how get to the

10   Kennedy Boulevard. I didnt know where was it. I wanted to

11   help the young man anyway. I took the map from him and

12   find the Kennedy Boulevard. But I didnt know how explain

13   the directions to him. So I walked with him to there. The

14   next day was first day of school. I went to my english class

15   and sat down. There was the same young man! He was

16   student just like me. Now we're freinds.

Most editors use editing marks. You will use these marks to edit your own final drafts:

Editing Mark	Example
∧ Add	It was ∧ day after . . . (*the* added above)
— Take out	~~the~~ Kennedy Boulevard
≈ Put capital letter	e̲n̲glish
/ Put small letter	the United States ∅f America
⌐ Transpose	I didn't know where was⌐it
	fre⌐i⌐nds
∧̦ Add comma	He was a student∧̦ just like me.
⊙ Add period	. . . the day after I arrived in the U̲S̲⊙.
∨̇ Add apostrophe	I still didṅt understand.
∨̈ Add quotation marks	I . . . told him,̈ I do not understand.̈
agr Make verb agree with subject	*agr* He go to American College.
vf Change verb form	*vf* I knew he is a foreigner.
Sp Change spelling	*Sp* campόs

In-Class Practice: Note the Differences

Read Nicolas's final draft with editing marks. Then read his edited draft on page 33. What corrections did Nicolas make? Finish the chart below:

line 1   *the* before *day* // *the* before *U.S.* // period in *U.S.*

     2   *campos* → *campus* // *the* → *a*

     3   take out *be*

     4

     5

     6

     7

     8

     9

10

11

12

13

14

15

16

Read Nicolas's explanation of his editing process:

Nicolas: I read my final draft one time. I checked verb forms first because I usually have trouble with them. Some of my verbs were in the present tense instead of the past tense. So I put "vf" above these verbs. Then I checked to see if the verbs in each sentence agreed with the subjects. They were all OK. Next I showed my final draft to Hiro. He found two misspelled words. We looked those words up in the dictionary. Hiro also told me to change *english* to *English*. Then I checked my articles. I needed to add *the* and *a* in a few places. I also needed to take out *the* before *Kennedy Boulevard.* Finally Hiro helped me with my punctuation.

Editing Exercises

At-Home Practice: Punctuation and Capitalization

Read the text below. Mark capital letters where they are needed. Mark periods at the ends of sentences, and mark other punctuation where it is needed. Use the editing marks on page 94. Look at Claire's edited draft in Chapter 3 to check your answers.

it is always hard to start a new way of life i came to the us when i

was 17 years old and i went to an american high school for one

year i knew it would be very hard for me to study in english but

i had no choice going to an american high school was exciting

but also very difficult everything was so strange to me in the

beginning i couldnt understand what my teachers said i even got

lost trying to find my classes i used to carry a dictionary with me all the time my classmates always watched me while i looked up

words in the dictionary the words were so easy for them but they

were new to me i felt so embarrassed i still used my dictionary

though because i wanted to learn new words that year i learned

two things pursue your goals dont worry about other peoples

opinions

In-Class Practice: Verb Forms, Subject/Verb Agreement, Articles, Spelling

The text below, "Shanghai," has four editing problems: spelling mistakes, missing articles, subject/verb agreement mistakes, and verb form mistakes.

1. Mark and correct these mistakes. Use the editing marks shown earlier in this chapter. Remember, there may be more than one mistake in a sentence.
2. Students write the sentences with corrections on the board.
3. Students explain their corrections.

Shanghai

Shanghai is largest city in China, but it is not the capitol. It have a

big population. The commerce there is very flurishing. From a map,

Shanghai look like a spider knet. People in Shanghai don't has

different names for street and avenue. They calling them both

"road." There is no maps with road index. So stranger who try to

travel in city without natives often gets lost.

Academic Journal Practice: Section 1

You worked on punctuation, capitalization, spelling, articles, subject/verb agreement, and verb forms. What was the most difficult for you to work on? Why? What was the easiest for you? Why?

Edit Your Final Drafts

You will now edit your final drafts.

Field-of-Study Report

At-Home Practice: Editing by Yourself

Reread and edit the final draft of your "Field-of-Study" report.

1. Read once to mark and correct punctuation and capitalization mistakes.
2. Read a second time to mark and correct spelling mistakes and to add and take out articles.
3. Read a third time to mark and correct subject/verb agreement and verb form problems.

In-Class Practice: Group Editing

1. Make two photocopies of your "Field-of-Study" final draft with your corrections. Bring these copies to class.
2. Get into a group with two other students. Distribute the copies of your final draft.
3. Reread your draft silently. You and the group members will look for more mistakes in punctuation, capitalization, spelling, articles, subject/verb agreement, and verb forms.
4. Discuss with the group members how to correct the mistakes. Use your dictionaries and grammar handbooks. If you have any difficulty, ask your teacher.
5. Repeat this process with each group member's final draft.

At-Home Practice: Recopying

Carefully recopy the final draft of your report. Include all the corrections. Give this edited draft to your teacher to check. After she returns it, put it in your Writing Folder.

In-Class Practice: Discussion About Group Editing

How did the group help you? What was the difference between editing by yourself and group editing? Discuss your answers with the class.
  Hiro wanted to edit this final draft:

Staying Alive

Most important thing for the humans is staying alive. We cant imagene dying. The doctors and the sientists look for ways to keep

us alive. They have machines, surgery and medecine to postpone

death. But the doctors cant keep us alive foreaver. They can only

give us some more years of health and life.

Hiro asked Claire to help him with his biggest problem—articles. He asked Anatoly to check the verbs and Fatema to check the spelling, punctuation, and capitalization. Here is their conversation:

Fatema: I only found four spelling mistakes: *imagine, scientists, medicine,* and *forever.*

Anatoly: I didn't find any verb problems. Should I look again?

Hiro: No, thanks. I checked the verbs carefully before. I think they are all correct.

Claire: Well, I found some mistakes! You need to work on the articles. Let's read each sentence and add and take out articles.

At-Home Practice: Editing Exercise

Edit Hiro's draft.

"Observation" Paper

At-Home Practice: Editing by Yourself

Reread and edit the final draft of your "Observation" paper.

1. Read once to mark and correct punctuation and capitalization mistakes.
2. Read a second time to mark and correct spelling mistakes and to add and take out articles.
3. Read a third time to mark and correct subject/verb agreement and verb form problems.

In-Class Practice: Group Editing

1. Make three photocopies of your "Observation" final draft with your corrections. Bring these copies to class.
2. Get into a group with three other students. Distribute the copies of your final draft.
3. One student will mark and correct punctuation and capitalization mistakes. Another student will mark and correct spelling mistakes

and add and take out articles. The other student will mark and correct subject/verb agreement and verb form problems.

4. Repeat this process with each group member's final draft.

At-Home Practice: Recopying

Carefully recopy the final draft of your observation paper. Include all the corrections. Give this edited draft to your teacher to check. After she returns it, put it in your Writing Folder.

"First Impressions" Story

In-Class Practice: Editing Chart

1. Bring the final draft of your "First Impressions" story to class.

2. Edit your final draft. Then recopy it.

3. Count the mistakes. How many punctuation, capitalization, spelling, and other mistakes did you make?

4. Look at Hiro's editing chart on page 100. Then fill in the editing chart on page 101.

5. Give your editing chart and your edited story to your teacher to check. After she returns them, put them in your Writing Folder.

Choose Titles

Ling decided to put her "First Impressions" story in the class magazine. She needed to choose a title for her story. She wrote four possible titles in her Academic Journal: "Sending a Package," "Waiting at the Post Office," "Misunderstanding at the Post Office," and "First Trip to the Post Office." Then Ling chose one of these titles. Which of these titles do you like best for her story? Why? Reread Ling's edited draft in Chapter 3 to help you decide.

Academic Journal Practice: Section 1

1. Reread the edited draft of your "First Impressions" story. Write down three or four titles for this story. Choose one of these titles and write it at the top of your story.

2. Repeat this process for your "Observation" and "Field-of-Study" papers.

3. Put the three papers back in your Writing Folder.

Editing Chart

Name _Hiro_

Date _Nov. 15_

Title of Paper _Staying Alive_

	Number of Mistakes
Spelling	4
Articles	5
Punctuation	2
Verb Forms	0
Capitalization	0
Subject/Verb Agreement	0

Comments: _My biggest problem is articles. When do I add the or take the? When do I use a? Everything else is ok. Maybe I need to work on my spelling_

Editing Chart

Name

Date

Title of Paper

Number of Mistakes

Spelling _____

Articles _____

Punctuation _____

Verb Forms _____

Capitalization _____

Subject / Verb Agreement _____

Comments: _____

_____

_____

_____

_____

_____

_____

_____

_____

_____

_____

Tear out this sheet and give it to your teacher with your edited story.

Create a Class Magazine

At-Home Practice: Choosing a Paper for the Magazine

Reread your three edited drafts. Pick your favorite one. This paper will go in the class magazine. Give your paper to your teacher. She will ask some students to help her make the class magazine.

Language Tale 3

Kimiko needed help with her first draft, so she went to see her teacher. She gave him her draft and he began to read it silently. After a few moments, Kimiko asked, "Do you have a red pen?" He answered no, so she looked in her bookbag for one. "Here," she said, handing a red pen to her teacher. "You can use this." He thanked her, put the pen on his desk, and continued to read.

Why did Kimiko give the pen to her teacher? Why did he put it on the desk? Do you think Kimiko's teacher did the right thing? Why or why not?

Final Draft of "My Own Topic"

Maria used her teacher's comments to write a final draft of her paper about the way American students dress. Then she edited her final draft and she chose a title:

Dressing for Class

In hot weather American students wear shorts to class. In cold weather they wear jeans and sweaters. Both men and women students wear jeans to class. American professors don't mind that their students dress informally.

In my country, on the other hand, the professors prefer formal dress in the classroom. So the women students wear dresses to class and the men students wear trousers and shirts. Some students in my country want to dress like American students. They wear jeans, T-shirts, and sneakers to class. But most students still dress formally.

Read Maria's second draft in Chapter 6. Read her teacher's comments in Chapter 6. How did Maria use her teacher's comments to write her final draft? Use your teacher's comments to write the final draft of "My

Own Topic." Put this final draft in your Writing Folder. In Chapter 9 you will edit this final draft and choose a title for it.

Summary

In this chapter you learned to use editing marks, and you edited final drafts by yourself and in a group. You also helped other students edit their final drafts. You chose titles for your edited drafts, and you picked one of these edited drafts for the class magazine.

UNIT THREE

Writing About Reading

In the next three chapters, you will use writing to help you read and understand texts. You will take notes, write summaries, and write a short essay.

CHAPTER 8

Taking Notes

In this chapter
—You will learn strategies for taking notes from readings and discussions. To be a successful student you must be able to take good notes. Taking good notes will help you study and learn.

This chapter is about taking notes from readings and discussions. But taking notes is not a new activity for you. In Chapter 4 you took notes about the place you observed. In Chapter 6 you took notes about your field of study. In this chapter you will take notes while reading and while discussing your reading with your classmates. This work will prepare you to read textbooks and take lecture notes.

Learn About Taking Notes from Reading

Taking Notes from Readings

Students take notes to remember, to think on paper, and to learn.
How to take good notes from readings:

1. Read the text once to find out what the text is about.
2. Then reread the text. As you reread mark the words or groups of words:
   —that seem important to you
   —that you do not understand
   —that you have questions about

   In the margins of the text jot down comments and questions about the marked words.
3. Then look up new vocabulary in the dictionary.

Naturally, if the text does not belong to you, you cannot make marks on it. Copy words and take notes on a separate sheet of paper.

Anatoly's teacher gave the class the following text to read:

THE BOOTSTRAP PROGRAM

The first computer designers had to solve a problem: How do you teach computers to read programs? If you give Program A to a computer to teach it to read all other programs, how does it read Program A?

Think of the problem in these terms: You are five years old and just starting school. A slick salesman comes by your house with a book he claims will teach you how to read in two weeks. Your mom, ever alert to rip-offs, asks, "But if my child can't read, what's she going to do with this book?"

Now imagine yourself in a different way: born with that salesman's book already *in your brain*. That would mean that as soon as you could pick up a book you could read it.

Computer designers found a similar solution to their problem. They designed the computer with a *built-in* program (the "bootstrap program") to tell it how to read other programs. The bootstrap program is part of the operating system, the set of programs that tell it how to be a computer. All computers have built-in operating systems.

When you turn on—or "boot up"—your computer, a series of things happens. First, the bootstrap program goes into place. Next, this program tells your computer how to read the rest of the operating system, and then this whole system goes into place. Now the computer is ready to act like a computer.

The terms *boot up* and *bootstrap program* are actually metaphors in computerese. They probably derive from the saying "to pull yourself up by your bootstraps."

Study Different Notetaking Styles

Anatoly read the text once and then he reread it. As he reread he marked the words and groups of words (1) that he thought were important, (2) that he did not understand, and (3) that he had questions about. In the margins he jotted down comments and questions. Here is the same text, with Anatoly's notes:

THE BOOTSTRAP PROGRAM– *?*

The first computer designers had to solve a problem: How do you teach computers to read programs? If you give <u>Program A to a computer to teach it to</u> *How do computer read* <u>read</u> all other programs, how does it read Program A?

slick? Think of the problem in these terms: You are five years old and just starting school. A <u>slick</u> salesman comes by your house with a book he <u>claims</u> will *claims* teach you how to read in two weeks. Your mom, ever alert to <u>rip-offs</u>, asks, *rip-offs* "But if my child can't read, what's she going to do with this book?"

Now imagine yourself in a different way: born with that salesman's book already *in your brain*. That would mean that as soon as you could pick up a book you could read it. *The book in my brain teaches me to read all books Great!*

Computer designers found a similar solution to their problem. They designed the computer with a <u>*built-in* program</u> (the "bootstrap program") to tell *built-in program "bootstrap program"* <u>it how to read other programs</u>. <u>The bootstrap program is part of the operating system</u>, the set of programs that tell it how to be a computer. All computers *part of operating system* have built-in operating systems. *boot up = turn on where does boot up come from?*

When you <u>turn on</u>—or "<u>boot up</u>"—your computer, a series of things *like paragraph* happens. First, the bootstrap program goes into place. Next, <u>this program</u> *the program* <u>tells your computer how to read the rest of the operating system</u>, and then *tells computer how to read* this whole system goes into place. Now the computer is ready to act like a computer.

computerese? The terms *boot up* and *bootstrap program* are actually <u>metaphors in</u> *metaphors?* <u>computerese</u>. They probably derive from the saying "to pull yourself up by <u>your bootstraps</u>." *An American saying? a proverb? sounds like Chinese What does it mean?*

In-Class Practice: Studying One Notetaking Style

Reread "The Bootstrap Program" text with Anatoly's notes. Next, write your answers to the questions below. Then discuss your answers with the whole class.

1. Anatoly marked some words because he did not know their definitions. Find at least two of these words and write them here:

_____

What do the words mean?

2. Anatoly marked some groups of words because they seemed important to him. Find one of these groups. Write it here: _____

_____

Does this group of words seem important to you? Why or why not?

3. Find one of Anatoly's questions. What should he do to answer this question?

4. What words in "The Bootstrap Program" do *you* want to mark? Why?

Academic Journal Practice: Section 1

Here are some of Patricia's and Chung's notes on "The Bootstrap Program." Compare them to Anatoly's notes. How are the three notetaking styles different? How are they the same?

Patricia's Notes:

_____

THE BOOTSTRAP PROGRAM

Computer designers found a similar solution to their problem. They designed the computer with a built-in program (the "bootstrap program") to tell it how to read other programs. The bootstrap program is part of the operating system, the set of programs that tell it how to be a computer. All computers have built-in operating systems.

When you turn on—or "boot up"—your computer, a series of things happens. First, the bootstrap program goes into place. Next, this program

like T.V. sets! What is "act like a computer!"

tells your computer how to read the rest of the operating system, and then) this whole system(goes into place.) Now the computer is ready(to act like a computer.) *What place !*

Chung's Notes:

THE BOOTSTRAP PROGRAM

Computer designers found a similar solution to their problem. They de- *how to teach c.s to read* *progra*
signed the computer with a[*built-in*]program (the "bootstrap program") to tell it how to read other programs. The bootstrap program is part of the operating system, the set of programs that tell it how to be a computer. All computers have[built-in]operating systems. *how to read, add, subtract, etc*

When you turn on—or ["boot up"]—your computer, a series of things happens. First, the bootstrap program goes into place. Next, this program tells your computer how to read the rest of the operating system, and <u>then</u> this whole system goes into place. Now the computer is ready <u>to act like a computer.</u>

Take Notes from Reading

At-Home Practice: Taking Your Own Notes

Turn to Appendix A. You will find three texts there. Which text do you want to read? Tear it out. Write the title here: _____

_____ This is your text.

Now, read your text once. Next, reread it and take notes. Later in this chapter you will discuss your text and compare your notes with some classmates'.

Academic Journal Practice: Section 1

Was your text difficult or easy to read? Why? Was taking notes difficult or easy? Why? Did taking notes help you understand your text better?

Learn About Taking Notes from Discussions

Taking Notes from Discussions

Students take notes during discussions to record the speakers' ideas and to record their own comments and questions about those ideas.

How to take good notes from discussions:

1. Jot down the speakers' ideas. Write just the *key words*—the most important words you hear. Don't try to write down all the words.

2. Write your comments and questions about the speakers' ideas.

Anatoly, Patricia, and Chung formed a group to discuss "The Bootstrap Program." Here is part of their discussion:

Anatoly: What's a program?

Chung: I know. A program tells the computer what to do.

Patricia: You mean, like instructions?

Chung: Yeah. It tells the computer, "Do this, then do this, then do this, then do this. . . ."

Anatoly: That reminds me of my mother. She always tells me what to do!

Patricia: It's not the same thing.

Chung: Yeah, that's right. People aren't like computers.

Patricia: And computers aren't like people.

Anatoly: But it says here that the bootstrap program tells your computer how to read. *People* read. How do *computers* read?

Chung: Computers don't read like people read.

Patricia: So, how do computers read?

Chung: Well . . . I'm not sure . . . but a computer has to know how to read first. Then it can read programs.

Anatoly took notes during the discussion. Here are some of his notes:

> 4/12 discussion of "Bootstrap
> Program" with Chung and Patricia
> program
> instructions   (Mother!)

computers ≠ people

how do computers read ??

Bootstrap program
1. Know how to read
{ 2. read programs
what are some other programs?

At-Home Practice: Studying Anatoly's Discussion Notes

Reread the students' discussion of "The Bootstrap Program" and Anatoly's discussion notes. What key words from the discussion did Anatoly
write? What questions about the discussion did he write?

Take Discussion Notes

In-Class Practice: Discussing Your Text and Taking Notes

Bring your text to class. Form a group with two or three classmates with
the same text as yours. Compare your notes. Discuss your text. Take
notes during the discussion. In the next chapter you will use all your
notes to help you write a summary of your text.

Academic Journal Practice: Section 1

What did you learn from the discussion about your text?

Give your Academic Journal to your teacher. He will read it, write
comments, and return the journal to you.

More Writing on Your "Brainstorming" Topic

In Chapter 6, you used the ideas you got from brainstorming to write a
first draft. Bring this first draft to class. Get together with two other
students. Share your first drafts and then respond. Tell the writer:

1. What you remember

2. What you like

3. What you want to know more about

Fill out Response Sheet E on page 115. Use Response Sheet E to revise your first draft. Then give your second draft and Response Sheet E to your teacher. He will write comments on your draft. In the next chapter you will write a final draft of this paper.

Summary

In this chapter you studied different notetaking styles. You also took notes while reading and while discussing texts.

Response Sheet E: "Brainstorming" Topic

Name

Date

My group members:

My group remembered:

My group liked:

My group wanted to know more about:

Other comments:

CHAPTER 9

Summaries

In this chapter
—You will learn to summarize texts. Summarizing, like taking good notes, will help you study and learn.

At the end of each chapter of this book there is a *summary* of the chapter. The summaries tell, very briefly, what you did in the chapters. You wrote some summaries yourself. On Response Sheet A you wrote a summary of your partner's first draft ("My partner's first draft is about. . . ."). On Response Sheet B you summarized the first drafts of your classmates' observation papers ("What did the writer tell me about this place?"). In this chapter you will summarize your text from Appendix A.

Summarizing Readings

Summarizing a text means writing a brief statement of the main ideas of that text. Students write summaries of texts to help them understand those texts.

How to summarize a text:

1. Use your notes to help you find the author's main ideas.

2. Explain these main ideas very briefly. Use your own words.

3. Never copy the author's sentences in your summary. But you may use some key words from the text.

Compare Three Summaries

Anatoly used all his notes to help him write a summary of "The Bootstrap Program." Here is his summary:

A Bootstrap Program is something in the computer. It is built-in. The Bootstrap Program is important because it tells the computer how to read. Then the computer can read other programs and do the things you want it to do. Without the Bootstrap Program the computer couldn't do anything. "Bootstrap Program" comes from "to pull yourself up by your bootstraps" ("to help yourself").

Here is Patricia's summary of the same text:

Computers read programs to tell them what to do. All computers have a

> built-in program. It tells them
> how to read the other programs. This
> built-in program is called "the
> bootstrap program."

And here is Chung's summary:

> Computer engineers designed computers
> with built — in operating systems. A comp
> —uter's operating systems contains
> instructions for the computer. One set
> of these instructions tells the computer
> how to read other programs. This set
> of instructions is the Bootstrap program.

In-Class Practice: Comparing the Students' Summaries

Reread all three summaries. How are they similar? How are they different? Tell the class.

Write a Summary

At-Home Practice: Writing a Summary of Your Text

Reread your notes about your text from Appendix A. Then, summarize your text. Attach your summary to your text with notes. Then put both in your Writing Folder.

Academic Journal Practice: Section 1

Do you still have questions and comments about your text? Write them in your journal.

Take Notes and Summarize

More Practice in Taking Notes and Summarizing

1. Turn to Appendix A. Choose one of the two remaining texts and tear it out. Which text did you choose? Write the title here:

   _____ This is your text. Now, read your text once. Next, reread it and take notes.

2. Bring your text to class. Form a group with two or three classmates with the same text as yours. Compare your notes. Discuss your text. Take notes during the discussion.

3. Reread all your notes. Summarize your text. Attach your summary to your text with notes and put them both in your Writing Folder.

In-Class Practice: Vocabulary Exercise D

Each student chooses one or two new words from her Academic Journal and tells them to the teacher. The teacher writes the words on the board. Which words do you know? What do they mean? Tell the class. The teacher will write the definitions on the board.

Copy the words from the board onto Vocabulary Exercise Chart D. Copy the definitions, too.

Vocabulary Exercise Chart D

Word	Definitions
_____	_____
	_____
	_____
_____	_____
	_____
	_____
_____	_____
	_____

_____   _____

_____   _____

_____   _____

_____   _____

_____   _____

_____   _____

_____

Academic Journal Practice: Section 2

Copy Vocabulary Exercise Chart D into the vocabulary section of your Academic Journal.

Editing and Choosing a Title for "My Own Topic"

1. Reread and edit the final draft of your "My Own Topic" paper.
2. Make three photocopies of this final draft with your corrections. Bring these copies to class for group editing.
3. Get into a group with three other students. Distribute the copies.
4. One student will mark and correct punctuation and capitalization mistakes. Another student will mark and correct spelling mistakes and add and take out articles. The other student will mark and correct subject/verb agreement and verb form problems.
5. Repeat this process with each group member's final draft.
6. Choose a title for your edited draft.
7. Recopy your edited draft carefully. Write the title at the top.
8. Put this edited draft in your Writing Folder.

More Writing on Your "Brainstorming" Topic

1. Reread Response Sheet E from your partners. Read your teacher's comments on your second draft.
2. Revise your second draft. This new draft will be your final draft.
3. Edit your final draft.
4. Choose a title for your edited draft.
5. Recopy your edited draft carefully. Put the title at the top.
6. Put the edited draft in your Writing Folder.

Give your Writing Folder to your teacher. She will read your summaries, the edited draft of your "Brainstorming" paper, and the edited draft of "My Own Topic."

Language Tale 4

Michael got an assignment to write an essay about the life and work of Gandhi. He went to the library and checked out a book about Gandhi. Then he went to his dorm room, sat down at his desk, and began to copy out of the book. Michael's roommate asked, "What are you doing?"

"Writing a paper about Gandhi," answered Michael.

"You can't copy whole sentences out of the book to write your paper," said his roommate. "That's plagiarism."

"But I have to copy," Michael said. "I don't know anything about Gandhi."

What should Michael do to learn about Gandhi? How can he write the paper? What is plagiarism?

Summary

In this chapter you read and wrote summaries of texts. You took more notes while reading and while discussing texts.

CHAPTER 10

Short Essay

In this chapter
—You will use the writing strategies described in this book to write a short essay. Writing essays is a requirement for many college courses.

In Chapters 3 through 7 you learned to freewrite, brainstorm, revise, and edit. In Chapters 8 and 9 you learned to take notes and summarize. Now you will use these strategies to write a short essay about a text called "America: The Car Society."

Write Before Reading

In-Class Practice: Initial Writing

What do you know about the topic, "America: The Car Society"? To find out, answer these questions before you read the text. Write your answers in Section 3 of your Academic Journal.

1. What are my first thoughts about this topic?

2. What are my experiences with this topic?

3. What is difficult about this topic for me?

4. What do I want to know about this topic?

Read, Take Notes, and Summarize

Academic Journal Practice: Section 3

Read "America: The Car Society." While you read, take notes in the margins. When you finish, summarize it in your Academic Journal.

AMERICA: THE CAR SOCIETY

In the United States today, there are more than 100 million cars on the road, almost one for every two Americans. It's difficult to imagine what the United States would be like without the car and all its accompanying developments. In many ways, our life has been affected by the car so much that we could not do without it. As Bill Moyers put it, the car "gave us mobility, romance, freedom, status, jobs, and required in return only that we come utterly to depend on it."[1]

Our utter dependence on the car brought us problems as well as benefits. With mobility, romance, freedom, status, and jobs, we got poor public transportation, suburban sprawl, 55,000 highway deaths yearly, pollution, and the deterioration of the inner city.

Cars made it possible for people to live in suburbs and commute to work. After World War II, white-collar workers moved out of the cities, leaving blue-collar workers and the unemployed to fend for themselves. City shops and department stores lost business to huge suburban malls. As a result, suburbs flourished while the cities declined.

The U.S. government contributed to the growth of suburban life by funding and constructing the largest system of roads and bridges in the world. Across the country, scenery changed as the landscape was blasted and leveled to make way for roads connecting cities to outlying suburbs. Yet public transportation in and between cities was almost completely ignored. The argument between funding public transportation and funding highway systems can go on for years. New York City, for example, battled for ten years about a proposed 4.2-mile highway for commuters in Manhattan. Some citizens argued that the money should go for the subway system, which is badly in need of repair. Finally, funding was denied for this highway. Could this be the beginning of a trend to vote down support for highways connecting cities and suburbs?

When Americans see a car, we think too quickly of "the romance of the road." For most of us, the car means freedom to travel as far and as fast as we want. It means long highways through the lonesome desert or scenic mountains. Television advertisements for cars project this image; rarely do we see city traffic jams or cadillac ranches in these ads.[2] Most of us don't think of the pollution or wreckage or roadside eyesores that have come with the car. But if we wish to survive into the twenty-first century, we will have to develop ways to deal with the problems that the car has brought us. We may be totally dependent on the car, but we do not therefore have to allow it to bury us.

---

[1]PBS, "A Walk Through the 20th Century with Bill Moyers: America on the Road." June 1984.

---

[2]"Cadillac ranch" = auto dump for wrecked or old cars.

In-Class Practice: Group Discussion

In a group (three or four students), share your summary of the text with your group and discuss the text. Take notes on your group's discussion in Section 3 of your Academic Journal.

Freewrite

Academic Journal Practice: Section 3

1. Freewrite for fifteen minutes to answer this question: What do I know *now* about the topic, "America: The Car Society"?
2. Reread your initial writing, notes, summary, and freewriting. What sentences, phrases, and words in your writing seem interesting to you? Underline these.
3. Choose the three most interesting sentences, phrases, or words. Freewrite for ten minutes about each one. Then summarize each freewriting in one sentence.

   These summaries are ideas for your short essay. You will share these summary ideas with your classmates and then brainstorm about them.

   Jan chose one sentence from his initial writing and two sentences from his notes. Then he freewrote about each sentence and summarized his freewriting. Here are (a) one of his sentences from his notes, (b) the freewriting, and (c) the summary idea:

a) "My bike is my car."

b) I don't need a car – don't want a car – too much

trouble and too expensive.
I live 5 miles from school —
the bike is fine. But I
hate the traffic, especially
on the boulevard. They should
make streets for bikes —
no pollution, no noise.
People in cars make
difficulty for people on bikes.
Why? They should go to
work by bike. Everyday
I see many cars
with only one person inside.
They should drive together
or take the bus or get a
bike like me.

c) Summary^idea: There are too
many cars on the street.

Brainstorm

Jan brought his three summary ideas for his short essay to class. He brainstormed with Fatema and Hiro about the ideas. Here is part of their discussion:

Jan: My three ideas are: "There are too many cars on the streets," "Public transportation needs help from the government," and "Imagine the United States without cars."

Fatema: Which idea do you like best?

Jan: Well . . . I don't really know about the government and public transportation. I like the other two ideas most.

Hiro: Those two are similar. One says there are too many cars and the other is a dream about no cars.

Fatema: But it's an impossible dream. The United States is a car society.

Jan: But maybe that will change if everybody gets a bicycle. Like in Peking.

In-Class Practice: Brainstorming

1. With two or three classmates, brainstorm about your summary ideas. Take notes on your group's discussion. Ask each other these questions to start brainstorming:

   What is important about these ideas?

   What interests you most about these ideas?

   Which idea do you like best?

2. Which of your summary ideas do you want to write about? Write

   it here: _____

   _____ .

This is your essay topic.

Write a Short Essay

Jan decided to write about the advantages of bicycles in cities. Fatema decided to write about shopping malls. Here are their essays:

A Solution to Traffic Problems

City officials should forbid cars on city streets. There should only be public transportation such as subways, tramways, buses, and trains. People should walk or ride bicycles to work. In my opinion, the best kind of transportation is bicycles. Bicycles are clean and safe. They are not expensive. They don't need gas and they don't need much maintenance. Most people can repair their own bicycles. Bicycle riding is fun and excellent exercise, too. In Peking, for example, almost everyone rides a bicycle to work. There are very few cars on the streets and no parking problems there. Big cities should be like Peking.

Shopping at Malls

Many Americans prefer shopping at malls instead of shopping downtown. They don't want to spend time walking many city blocks from store to store. Shopping at malls is more convenient for them. They like to drive to the mall, park their cars, and shop in one large place. The clothing stores, food stores, jewelry stores, bookstores, record stores, and movie theaters are all next to each other under one big roof. Shoppers can spend the whole day at the mall. If they get hungry they can stop at a restaurant or a cafe. In the evening, they can see a film. Malls are American social centers. People meet, shop, and eat at malls.

Follow the procedure below to write your essay. The edited draft must be 100 to 200 words long. You will write this essay for your teacher and your classmates to read.

Procedure for Writing "Short Essay"

1. Reread your brainstorming notes about your summary ideas. Use these notes to write a first draft.
2. Share your first draft with two or three classmates. Write their responses on Response Sheet F.
3. Use your classmates' responses to revise your first draft. Give the second draft to your teacher for comments.
4. Use your teacher's comments to revise your second draft. Then edit it, choose a title, and recopy it. Put all the drafts and Response Sheet F in your Writing Folder.

Fill out Writing Questionnaire 2 on page 131. Put it in your Writing Folder. Then give your folder to your teacher. He will review all of your work for the term.

Summary

In this chapter you read a text, and you took notes on and summarized that text. Then you wrote a short essay using all the writing strategies described in this book. Finally, you filled out a second Writing Questionnaire.

Response Sheet F: "Short Essay"

Name

Date

Title of paper:

My group members:

My group remembered:

My group liked:

My group wanted to know more about:

Other comments:

Writing Questionnaire 2: Looking Back

Name _____

Date _____

1. Which paper did you enjoy writing most?

_____ First Impressions   _____ Short Essay

_____ Observation   _____ My Own Topic

_____ Field of Study   _____ Brainstorming

   Why?

2. Which paper was most difficult for you? Why?

3. What did you learn about writing this term?

Appendix A

Texts for
Chapters 8 and 9

ECONOMICS: INTEREST

Jersey Gilbert

Interest is the price of money. It may seem strange to speak of money having a price. After all, a thousand dollars is worth a thousand dollars. Why should one have to pay more to get the thousand dollars? The answer is, if a borrower wants someone else to give up money, that borrower has to offer some reward. People won't lend money if there is no gain.

Of course, some people give money away as charity just as some farmers give surplus vegetables to their friends and neighbors. But, in general, one has to pay farmers for the trouble involved in growing more vegetables than they wish to eat themselves. In the same way, one has to pay people for the trouble involved in saving sums of money large enough to lend.

There is another parallel between the lender and the farmer. The price paid to the farmer for his vegetables has to cover the possibility that there will be no harvest due to bad weather or other troubles. Similarly, the price paid to a lender has to cover the possibility that some borrowers may not pay the interest or return the loan.

LITERATURE: VOICE

Peter Oberlink

When we read a poem or a story it seems that a voice is speaking to us through the words on the page. This voice describes places and things to us, tells us about certain events, and reports what characters say to one another. Sometimes the speaker behind the voice refers to himself as "I." At other times the speaker never refers to himself.

In order to understand a poem or a story better, it helps to ask, "What voice do I hear speaking as I read?" Of course the author creates the voice. But this does not mean that we hear the author's personal voice. The voice may resemble the author's personal voice very much, but it can also be very different. The voice may be young or very old, cheerful or melancholy. The voice may be consistent and truthful or it may be mischievous and tell small lies. It can be proud, humble, cowardly, brave, gentle, excited, or any combination of things. In other words, the voice is a fictional device that the author uses to present his subject matter. By attending to the voice, we can learn about the way the speaker behind the voice looks at the world.

ECOLOGY: WETLANDS

Jane Benesch

Millions of acres of land in the continental United States are covered by bogs, swamps, and marshes. These areas are called wetlands. A wetland is a transition site between water and land.

Wetlands act as a natural habitat for many plants and animals. For example, about 80 percent of commercial fish and shellfish depend on wetlands for their survival, and many endangered plant species are found only in wetlands. Wetlands can also improve the quality of the water surrounding them. They absorb polluted water, purify it, and release it in a form less harmful to aquatic life.

Until recently, wetlands were thought of as worthless lands. A study conducted by the U.S. Fish and Wildlife Service shows that between the mid-1950s and mid-1970s, an average of 458,000 acres of wetlands were lost each year to agricultural, urban, and recreational development.

Since the early 1970s, federal and state laws have been enacted to protect wetlands. Despite these laws, however, the public remains largely unaware of the importance of these lands.

Sample Student Paper
with Teacher's Comments

This appendix includes a student's text written in response to an assignment to complete the language tale in Chapter 2, the teacher's comments
on the student's text, and an explanation of the teacher's comments.

When Jan saw a grocery store,
a record shop, a bank and a barber,
he soon understood that was not
the place which he was looking for
He decided to call Mike once again
and asked by the correct adress.
However. Jan heard the same
thing: "it is on the corner of $\underline{30}^{th}$
and Main". Jan was not desapointed.
He asked Mike to repeat again
and slowly. finally. Jan understood

I don't understand what you mean by disappointed. Do you mean that Jan was not happy, or do you mean that he was not surprised, or do you mean that he wasn't discouraged?

the correct adress:" on the corner of 13TH and Main". that's all right - Jan said. When Jan wanted to get a bus, He remember that he has no money. He decided to demmand someone. The first person whom whom he demmanded was an old woman. Infortunately she got ungry and she wanted to beat him. perhaps, she understood a very different thing! - "never mind" said Jan to himself. The second person whom He spoke was nice and symphactic girl. She was ready to help him She gave him the money.

Afterwards, Jan caught a bus and finally He arrived on Mike's Bike. Shop. He told (the story) Mike the story. Mike found it

To me, this means they didn't talk. If you mean that they talked for about 13-14 minutes, you need to write "They talked almost 15 minutes."

very fany and he laught began to laught at. Jan bought a nice bicycle and when he was retouring back he met the caled by Susanta ^ same nice and symphatic gire They talked almost talked 15 minuits. Jan made an appointment for the following weekend at the ~~Chinese Indian~~ chinese restaurant in the Lexington Avenue when the weekend arrived they had a lunch together and laterwards they left to attend a very interesting film. Since that date they became good friends.

Daniel –
   This is a good ending to Jan's story about buying a bicycle. The part about the old woman made me laugh. I like the other characters that you added – Mike and Susana seem very real. Also, you show that Jan had many other problems besides not being able to find the bike shop.
   Two things: <u>to demand</u> means to tell someone to do something. Did Jan demand money (did he say "give me some money") or did he ask for it (did he say "Please, would you give me some money?")? And <u>an appointment</u> is usually with

a doctor or a business person.
Maybe a better word is date — young
people go on dates with each other, so
maybe Jan made a date with Susana
for the following week. (Date can
also mean day of the week.)

Brief Analysis of the Text

Strengths: In this first draft Daniel has control of story elements (narration, chronological order, dialogue), and he is able to correctly use such connectors as *afterwards*, *finally*, and *however*. The text is a traditional story in that it contains crisis and resolution; yet it also shows imagination in the additional problems that Jan encounters (needing money, being misunderstood by the woman).

Weaknesses: Daniel has problems with spelling, prepositions, word choice (vocabulary), idiomatic expression, verb tense, syntax.

Explanation of the Teacher's Comments

In commenting on Daniel's draft, the teacher wanted to encourage him rather than correct what he had written. She used two techniques to encourage him to write more: (1) noting his successes and (2) asking questions about confusing parts.

The first paragraph of the teacher's final comment lists the successful parts of his essay, along with giving a personal response ("made me laugh"). Comments in the margins show where the teacher became confused and raise questions for Daniel to address in his revision. The second paragraph of the final comment points out words that are misused and can cause confusion ("demmand" and "apointement"). (Note that the teacher modeled the correct spellings of these words in her response.)

The teacher's comments may look lengthy, but writing them probably took no more time than correcting all the errors would have done. The teacher's almost chatty tone is meant to create and encourage dialogue between her and the student; she is an attentive reader responding to the meaning of Daniel's text. And even though the teacher has not commented on the other problems with Daniel's text, she would probably expect Daniel to spend time with his fellow students carefully editing a final draft of the text before handing it in to her for grading.

In other words, the teacher has established for herself and made clear to her students a hierarchy of concerns through her comments. At the top of the scale is addressing ideas in early drafts; at the bottom is focusing on correctness in the final draft.